In Chemo
Candid Conversations with God

By Elena A. Chevalier

PRESS

Dedication

This book is dedicated to my Lord and Savior Jesus Christ.

Thank You for choosing to come to earth as Emmanuel—God with us—in human form so that You might know by experience what it feels like to live in a frail body.

Thank You, my Savior, for the sacrifice You paid so that my sins could be forgiven.

Thank You for Your abundant mercy, grace, peace, and comfort that accompanied us during Our Journey through Cancer Land.

My Forever-Friend, I look forward to the time when we will share the joys and perfection of eternity together.

For Thou, God, hast been a strength to the poor,
a strength to the needy in his distress,
a refuge from the storm,
a shadow from the heat,
when the blast of the terrible ones
is as a storm against the wall.

Isaiah 25:4

Contents

Preface

The Battle to Believe

L ife is full of circumstances that scream, "God is mean!"

"If God allowed this to happen, how can you trust Him?"

"Hah! If that's the way God takes care of His children, who needs Him?"

"This Christian life isn't worth all the heartaches–give up on God."

There are many battles in life. But to me, the Battle to Believe is one of the fiercest battles we face as children of God.

But without faith it is impossible to please Him:
for He that cometh to God must believe that He is, and
that He is a rewarder of them that diligently seek Him.
Hebrews 11:6

Spiritually, it makes perfect sense that the biggest battles we face will have to do with who God is and whether it's worth it to serve Him. The issue of whether we believe

God is "worthy" of our love or "worthy" of our service is at the very core of living a life that is pleasing to Him and rewarding to us.

God clearly tells us that it is impossible to please Him if we don't believe that He is the merciful, gracious, loving, just, and kind God that He says He is. God said that it is impossible to please Him if we don't believe that He eagerly longs to reward those who lovingly seek Him.

Yet the fact is that many things in life seem to indicate the opposite. Health issues, problems with relationships, financial challenges, deaths of loved ones, and even the myriad day-to-day struggles we face can all chip away at our belief that God is good and that we can trust Him. But that's what faith is: believing God's Word even when it doesn't make sense to our finite minds. In this sin-filled, curse-laden world, the only way we can believe is by faith.

Now faith is the substance of things hoped for,
the evidence of things not seen.
Hebrews 11:1

Faith says, "God, even though I may not see it right now, I am going to keep on trusting that one day I will see that You are who You say You are. I am going to keep on trusting that it is worth it to love You and to serve You."

Faith is believing—even when you can't see it—that God is who the Bible says He is. He wants us to believe that He will reward us for believing Him and for diligently seeking Him.

May the pages of this book help you in your own personal Battle to Believe.

Introduction

Before our thirteen-year-old daughter began treatment for non-Hodgkin lymphoma, Burkitt's type, I knew I was going to need extra strength and encouragement from the Lord.

A friend of mine explained, "As mothers, we always would rather bear the pain and endure the sufferings than have our child go through it." Often what we feel for our children, she said, "is really worse than experiencing the pain yourself, because we are helpless and so used to being the fixer of our children's problems."

As I sought strength from the Lord, the idea came to me to look up positive statements that David and others had made in the book of Psalms. As I studied the more than one hundred verses that included the phrase "I will," I found myself writing meditations, prayers, and affirmations based on those verses.

The more I went to the Word of God for help, the more amazed I was to discover the wide spectrum of "I will" statements. Many of them tied in amazingly well with what we were going through and what I pictured other chemo patients going through.

Writing was my way of coping with my daughter's diagnosis and treatment. Along the way, though, the Lord placed in my mind the thought that my writings could be of value to other people.

In loving obedience to the Lord, I offer these thoughts, prayers, heart-cries, and dozens of verses, which I pray will be of benefit and blessing to those who yearn for understanding from our sometimes hard-to-fathom God.

You will notice that the words of this book reflect an open honesty that may not be typical of some people's relationship with God. In fact, these conversations may seem sacrilegious to some. But as Christians, our walk with God is supposed to be a personal relationship. I find it is far better for me to openly express my thoughts and feelings toward God, because He already knows what I am thinking anyway.

Psalm 77 is a good example of the type of open, honest thoughts that the devotions in this book reveal. Notice the deep struggles and questions about God that the author of this psalm shares:

I cried unto God with my voice,
Even unto God with my voice;
And he gave ear unto me.

In the day of my trouble I sought the Lord:
My sore ran in the night, and ceased not:
My soul refused to be comforted.

I remembered God, and was troubled:
I complained, and my spirit was overwhelmed.
Selah.
Thou holdest mine eyes waking:
I am so troubled that I cannot speak.

I have considered the days of old, the years of ancient
*   times.*
I call to remembrance my song in the night:

I commune with mine own heart:
And my spirit made diligent search.

Will the Lord cast off for ever?
And will he be favorable no more?
Is his mercy clean gone for ever?
Doth his promise fail for evermore?
Hath God forgotten to be gracious?
Hath he in anger shut up his tender mercies? Selah.

And I said, This is my infirmity:
But I will remember the years of the right hand of the most
    High.
I will remember the works of the Lord:
Surely I will remember thy wonders of old.
I will meditate also of all thy work, and talk of thy doings.

Thy way, O God, is in the sanctuary:
Who is so great a God as our God?
Thou art the God that doest wonders.
Psalm 77:1-14

The psalmist begs God for answers to some pretty tough questions. In the end, he is encouraged by remembering all the things the Lord has done for him in the past, in order to have strength to believe God and to go on in the future.

The book of Jeremiah also gives encouragement that we can have this type of freedom in our relationship with God when we are going through severe trials. This prophet loved the Lord he served, but when agonizing troubles came into his life, he couldn't refrain from telling God he wished he'd never been born.

Cursed be the day wherein I was born: let not the day
wherein my mother bare me be blessed... Wherefore

came I forth out of the womb to see labour and sorrow,
that my days should be consumed with shame?
Jeremiah 20:14-18

At one point, Jeremiah was in such despair that he even asked God if He was a liar. Jeremiah asked the Lord:

Why is my pain perpetual, and my wound incurable,
which refuseth to be healed? wilt thou be altogether
unto me as a liar, and as waters that fail? Jeremiah
15:18

God's response to Jeremiah's openness with Him is instructive. God does not reprove Jeremiah when he wishes he had never been born. But when the prophet apparently accuses God of being a liar and not keeping His promises, God replies:

Therefore thus saith the Lord, If thou return, then will
I bring thee again, and thou shalt stand before me:
and if thou take forth the precious from the vile, thou
shalt be as my mouth: let them return unto thee; but
return not thou unto them. Jeremiah 15:19

It appears that God is saying, "Jeremiah, if you return to trusting Me, then I can still use you as a prophet. But you've got to separate the crud of negative, critical thoughts from the gold of trusting Me. Trust the truths of My Word; your negative thinking and speaking will only draw you away from Me."

Through it all, though, God loved Jeremiah with an ever-lasting love.

The Lord hath appeared of old unto me, saying, Yea,
I have loved thee with an everlasting love: therefore

*with lovingkindness have I drawn thee. Jeremiah
31:3*

Jeremiah's interactions with God give me insights into
my prayer conversations with God. The Lord understands
that there are times when what I am saying is simply the cry
of a wounded heart reaching out to Daddy–Abba, Father–to
make it all better. At such times, I can sense His loving arms
comforting me.

Then there are times when my words cross the line into
belligerence, and I sense the disappointment of the Lord for
my faithlessness. Those are the times that I come to Him
asking for His forgiveness, grateful for His loving mercy.

That line between baring our soul and berating God is
an individual thing. God alone knows our hearts. God alone
determines what is acceptable, and He is perfectly able to
reveal the motive of our hearts to us. How thankful I am that
God patiently works with us through it all!

~ ~ ~

I found from my daughter's experience that the Journey
through Cancer Land is an up-and-down journey. Physically,
emotionally, and spiritually, there are days when you are
doing fine, yet the very next day you may be in the pit of
despair. On lots of days you simply feel overwhelmed by all
that has come into your life through this illness. It's hard to
keep focused.

This devotional book was written with these fluctuations
in mind.

When cancer and chemo threaten to wreak havoc with
your life and your body, and you don't know what to do
next, pick up this book and flip through the pages. Each
entry begins with one of the "I will" verses taken from the

book of Psalms. Reading the verse is important, because the devotion that follows is based on that verse.

Please note that this is not meant to be a book to teach doctrine. It is presented as a series of conversations between a person struggling with cancer and God. God's response is represented by the centered verses in italics.

As you join in on these conversation prayers with God, disregard those that you can't relate to and embrace those that resonate with the beat of your heart. Ample space is provided for you to take part in the conversations and record your own thoughts, comments, and prayers. Fold down corners of the pages you want to return to, or cross out the pages you can't stand.

Each person's Journey through Cancer Land is individual and unique. So feel free to read from the beginning to the end if you'd like, but the book also works well if you simply flip from page to page. Ask the Holy Spirit to guide you as you read.

May these devotions help you to see that the greatest blessing of this journey may be the deepening of your relationship with God. He is a Friend whose friendship you will cherish for eternity. Why not use this time to cultivate that friendship now?

Conversation

Devotions

GOD KNOWS IT ALL

Psalm 31:7 I will be glad and rejoice in thy mercy: for thou hast considered my trouble; thou hast known my soul in adversities.

I can't hide it, Lord. You see right through to the core of my very being. It's not very pretty now, is it? The anger and bitterness. The frustration and faithlessness. Yes, You have certainly known my soul in adversities.

But the mercy of the Lord
is from everlasting to everlasting
upon them that fear him.

And that's what amazes me about You. You understand. You don't slap me in the face or kick me in the rear. You don't zap me with a bolt of lightning when I'm tempted to curse You. Instead You love me. Even when I don't love myself. Even when I don't feel like I love You.

The Lord hath appeared of old unto me, saying,
Yea, I have loved thee
with an everlasting love:
therefore with lovingkindness have I drawn thee.

What an incredible God You are. Thank You for Your incredible mercy. Thank You for not giving me what I truly deserve. I can't rejoice in this situation I'm in; but God, I am glad for Your mercy.

Psalm 103:17   Jeremiah 31:3
The references at the end of each conversation refer to the italicized verses above.

COMFORT ME, LORD

Psalm 9:2 I will be glad and rejoice in thee: I will sing praise to thy name, O thou most High.

Lord, help me. I hurt. I'm scared. And I'm angry. But I don't want to be this way. I long for the days when things were normal.

As one whom his mother comforteth,
so will I comfort you.

I need Your help. Help me to remember that You are the God of Comfort, the God of Love, the God of Peace. Help me to remember that You are Emmanuel, which means "God with us."

Blessed be God,
even the Father of our Lord Jesus Christ,
the Father of mercies,
and the God of all comfort;
Who comforteth us in all our tribulation,
that we may be able to comfort them
which are in any trouble,
by the comfort wherewith we ourselves are
comforted of God.

Rearrange my thoughts so that the memories of Your greatness lift my spirit outside of the four walls that surround me. Only by Your power can I be glad and rejoice in You when everything inside me wants to scream in anger and agony.

Help me, Lord, so that I may be glad and rejoice in You.

Isaiah 66:13   Corinthians 1:3-4

SLEEPLESS NIGHTS

Psalm 4:8 I will both lay me down in peace, and sleep: for thou, Lord, only makest me dwell in safety.

When I close my eyes, Lord, sleep doesn't come. Sometimes fear keeps me awake; sometimes pain keeps me awake. Sometimes it's the big Unknown that haunts my thoughts in the darkness of night. Help me!

He [God] giveth his beloved sleep.

Help me to remember that only You make me to dwell in safety. Though physical problems may come, no one can invade the realm of spiritual union and comfort that I can have in You.

The eternal God is thy refuge,
and underneath
are the everlasting arms...

I will sleep in the knowledge that, waking or sleeping, You hold me in Your everlasting arms. Like David in the Bible, may I be able to say, *When I remember you on my bed, and think about you in the night watches. For you have been my help. I will rejoice in the shadow of your wings. My soul stays close to you. Your right hand holds me up. Psalm 63:6-8*

Psalm 127:2   Deuteronomy 33:27

FROM THE PITS

Psalm 7:17 I will praise the Lord according to his righteousness: and will sing praise to the name of the Lord most high.

Lord, my world is the pits right now. In the midst of this chemo, I can't find much to praise You about.

But as an act of my will, I can praise You for Your righteousness. I can praise You for who You are.

You are the Lord Most High, and I praise You because I know that You are sovereign. I believe that in Your loving wisdom and righteousness You have allowed this affliction in my life.

But the mercy of the Lord
is from everlasting to everlasting
upon them that fear him...

I may not feel like praising You, but by Your grace I will do it anyway. I know You understand.

Great is our Lord,
and of great power:
his understanding is infinite.
The Lord lifteth up the meek...

Psalm 103:17   Psalm 147:5-6

MY REFLECTION

Psalm 17:15 As for me, I will behold thy face in righteousness: I shall be satisfied, when I awake, with thy likeness.

When I look in the mirror, Lord, I am horrified by the face staring back at me. I am torn between not wanting to see what is happening to me and staring at the mirror trying to make sense of what I see there.

This has to change, Lord! I'm too obsessed with what I look like. Help me to focus more on Your face than on mine. Help me to gaze into Your loving eyes through the words of Scripture.

Sometimes I'm tempted to think I won't be satisfied until my hair has grown back and other things return to normal. But help me to come to the point of being satisfied when I reflect You.

Behold, what manner of love
the Father hath bestowed upon us,
that we should be called the sons of God...

Beloved, now are we the sons of God,
and it doth not yet appear what we shall be:
but we know that, when he shall appear,
we shall be like him; for we shall see him as he is.

May Psalm 17:15 be true of me. Help me to forget myself. Help others to see Jesus in me, and I shall be satisfied.

1 John 3:1-2

FORGOTTEN WORKS OF GOD

Psalm 9:1 I will praise thee, O Lord, with my whole heart; I will shew forth all thy marvellous works.

Whoa, Lord. I had almost forgotten. In the midst of all the junk I am dealing with, I had forgotten that You have done so many marvelous things in the past.

Do I believe that You will continue to do wonderful things in the future? I'm not even sure there is a future for me here on earth.

The works of the Lord are great,
sought out of all them that have pleasure therein.
His work is honourable and glorious:
and his righteousness endureth for ever.
He hath made his wonderful works to be remembered:
the Lord is gracious and full of compassion.

I need You to help me remember times in the past when You have worked in wonderful ways. I need You to bring my thoughts back into line with the awesome truth of Your incredible power. I need You to restore the hope that in the midst of this physical misery, You are able to do marvelous things.

It's the only way I can endure.

Psalm 111:2-4

THE AGONY OF NOT KNOWING

Psalm 9:14 That I may shew forth all thy praise in the gates of the daughter of Zion: I will rejoice in thy salvation.

Lord, there's so much I don't know. Sometimes I think I will go crazy from the agony of not knowing. Of waiting. Of wondering. Of worrying.

But regardless of all that is going on around me, there is one thing I know I can cling to as I would to a rock in a raging sea. I know without a doubt that I am Your child.* I can rejoice in Your salvation.

And I give unto them eternal life;
and they shall never perish,
neither shall any man pluck them out of my hand.
My Father, which gave them me,
is greater than all;
and no man is able to pluck them
out of my Father's hand.

I know that, because I have asked Jesus to be my Savior, You have forgiven all my sins. One day I will rejoice in Your presence in heaven. It is the one thing for which I am certain in this uncertain world. One day, all the sorrow and pain and suffering of this earth will be over.

[I]n thy [God's] presence is fulness of joy;
at thy right hand there are pleasures for evermore.

* See "Am I a Child of God?" in the back of the book.

John 10:28-29   Psalm 16:11

COUNTING BLESSINGS

Psalm 13:6 I will sing unto the Lord, because he hath dealt bountifully with me.

Despite all I am going through, I acknowledge that You have been generous with me, giving me more than I knew to ask for in the past.

I'm tempted to look at all the negatives, but when I begin to count my blessings I realize that I have been so blessed by You.

The blessing of the Lord,
it maketh rich,
and he addeth no sorrow with it.

It is amazing what a change in my spirit comes when I am discouraged, and I begin to count my blessings. I will sing and give You thanks for all the things with which I am blessed.

Blessed is the man whose strength is in thee.

For the Lord God is a sun and shield:
the Lord will give grace and glory:
no good thing will he withhold
from them that walk uprightly.

Help me to believe and see that You are my sun and shield when I go through the darkest of night.

Proverbs 10:22   Psalm 84:5   Psalm 84:11

IF YOU'RE SO GREAT, HOW COME I'M IN PAIN?

Psalm 145:5-6 I will speak of the glorious honour of thy majesty, and of thy wondrous works. And men shall speak of the might of thy terrible acts: and I will declare thy greatness.

Lord, I'm surrounded by pain and misery, tragedy and heartbreak. Sometimes it's hard to be hopeful.

I wonder, "Lord, if You're so great, how come I'm in so much pain?"

But I know that my circumstances don't change the fact that You are a great and awesome God. One day this episode of my life will all make sense to me.

Help me to really believe that.

But the God of all grace,

who hath called us unto his eternal glory by Christ Jesus,

after that ye have suffered a while,

make you perfect, stablish, strengthen, settle you.

I don't understand what You are doing and why You have to do it this way, but by Your grace, mercy, and peace, I believe You.

1 Peter 5:10

DECISIONS

Psalm 16:7 I will bless the Lord, who hath given me counsel.

Lord, there are just too many decisions to be made! I can't take it all in! I can't handle all the pressure and weight of not knowing what to do! I've never walked this path before, and I'm confused and frustrated!

I wake up during the night wondering what I should do. Then when I wake up in the morning, I begin again with the same questions and concerns just where I left off when I finally fell asleep.

Lord, I need You to guide me. I need You to give me wisdom. Guide me in making the right decisions.

For I know the thoughts that I think toward you,
saith the Lord,
thoughts of peace, and not of evil,
to give you an expected end.

Then shall ye call upon me,
and ye shall go and pray unto me,
and I will hearken unto you.
And ye shall seek me, and find me,
when ye shall search for me with all your heart.

When I lie awake at night wondering what to do, may You be the One who directs my thoughts and instructs me. I will bless You, O Lord, for I always have You to lead and guide me.

Jeremiah 29:11-13

TURNING TO GOD

Psalm 18:1-3 I will love thee, O Lord, my strength. The Lord is my rock, and my fortress, and my deliverer; my God, my strength, in whom I will trust; my buckler, and the horn of my salvation, and my high tower. I will call upon the Lord, who is worthy to be praised: so shall I be saved from mine enemies.

When I am overwhelmed, Lord, I am so glad I can turn to You. You are my strength; You are my rock and my fortress and my deliverer. You are my buckler (my shield) and my high tower. I will turn my heart towards You, Lord, and You will save me.

But now thus saith the Lord that created thee
and he that formed thee...,
Fear not: for I have redeemed thee,
I have called thee by thy name; thou art mine.
When thou passest through the waters, I will be with thee;
and through the rivers, they shall not overflow thee:
when thou walkest through the fire, thou
shalt not be burned;
neither shall the flame kindle upon thee.
For I am the Lord thy God, the Holy One of
Israel, thy Saviour
Since thou wast precious in my sight,
thou hast been honourable, and I have loved thee...
Fear not: for I am with thee.

Even though You won't make all the problems in my life disappear, I know that You will empower me to go through the struggles, strong in Your Spirit, protected and sheltered in Your love. I do love You, Lord.

Isaiah 43:1-5

MY INFLUENCE ON OTHERS

Psalm 22:22, 25 I will declare thy name unto my brethren: in the midst of the congregation will I praise thee... My praise shall be of thee in the great congregation: I will pay my vows before them that fear him.

Lord, help me to be willing to share Your love and blessings with others. Many people might say, "A wise and loving God wouldn't permit people to suffer from cancer," and for that reason they don't believe in You. But I know that You are good and loving.

Lord, I know that it is hard for others to see Your love when they see me suffering. Help me to think of their needs and not just my own. Give me wisdom how I can encourage others who are discouraged by my condition.

Ye are my witnesses, saith the Lord,
and my servant whom I have chosen:
that ye may know and believe me,
and understand that I am he...
I, even I, am the Lord;
and beside me there is no saviour.

Use me, Lord, to demonstrate Your power and love and mercy. May my example never cause others to turn away from You.

Easy words to say, but without Your power, my efforts are worthless. You've got to do Your part, or this situation is hopeless. Strengthen me, Lord, to praise You before others.

Fear ye not, neither be afraid:
have not I told thee from that time, and have
declared it?
ye are even my witnesses...

Isaiah 43:10, 11   Isaiah 44:8

THE WORDS OF MY MOUTH

Psalm 34:1 I will bless the Lord at all times: his praise shall continually be in my mouth.

Lord, as an act of my will, I choose to consecrate my mouth to You.

Help me to have only words of praise and positive things in my mouth. *Let the words of my mouth, and the meditation of my heart, be acceptable in thy sight, O Lord, my strength, and my redeemer. Psalm 19:14*

I want to bless You at all times, not just when things are going well, and not just when things are going my way. I want to praise and bless Your name regardless of the circumstances.

Fear thou not;
for I am with thee:
Be not dismayed; for I am thy God:
I will strengthen thee;
yea, I will help thee;
Yea, I will uphold thee
with the right hand of my righteousness.

By Your grace, this is my goal: that praising You will flow as easily from my lips as complaining did in the past.

Isaiah 41:10

OVERWHELMED BY PEOPLE

Psalm 3:6 I will not be afraid of ten thousands of people, that have set themselves against me round about.

Lord, sometimes it seems that there are so many people, people, people, people wanting to poke and prod me.
When I am overwhelmed by the number of people involved in this whole process, help me to remember that these people are here for our greatest good.

Thou wilt keep him in perfect peace,

> *whose mind is stayed on thee:*
> *because he trusteth in thee.*

> *Trust ye in the Lord for ever:*
> *for in the Lord Jehovah is*
> *everlasting strength.*

By Your power at work in me, I will not be afraid or unsettled or alarmed at the continual parade of people.
By your grace, I will be at peace. Keep me in Your perfect peace—I can't do it alone.

Isaiah 26:3-4

LIES I REFUSE TO BELIEVE

Psalm 23:6 Surely goodness and mercy shall follow me all the days of my life: and I will dwell in the house of the Lord for ever.

The bottom line is, Lord, I know that whatever happens I will be with You in eternity. Your goodness and Your mercy will follow me all the days of my life.

I will not believe the lie that because I have cancer, You are not good. I will not believe the lie that You won't forgive me for what I've done. I won't believe the lie that there is no hope.

> *But God commendeth his love toward us,*
> *in that, while we were yet sinners,*
> *Christ died for us.*

As an act of my will, I choose to believe that Jesus's sacrifice on the cross paid for my sins, that I am a child of Yours,* and that Your love, mercy, forgiveness, peace, strength, and help will be with me now and forever.

> *I, even I,*
> *am he that blotteth out*
> *thy transgressions*
> *for mine own sake,*
> *and will not remember thy sins.*

Romans 5:8   Isaiah 43:25

* See "Am I a Child of God?" at the end of the book.

FEELING ABANDONED BY GOD

Psalm 42:9 I will say unto God my rock, Why hast thou forgotten me? why go I mourning because of the oppression of the enemy?

Have You forgotten me, Lord?

Have You forgotten to hear me when I pray? Have You forgotten You promised to help me? Have You forgotten all the promises I've been clinging to, Lord?

You're supposed to me my Rock. You're supposed to protect me from the enemy. What happened, Lord?

I will keep asking You, my Rock, my Strength, until You give me some answers.

Oh, my Rock–my God, don't let me down now!

But Zion said, The Lord hath forsaken me,
and my Lord hath forgotten me.

[God replied,]

Can a woman forget her sucking child,
that she should not have compassion on
the son of her womb?
yea, they may forget,
yet will I not forget thee.
Behold, I have graven thee upon the
palms of my hands.

Isaiah 49:14-16

FALLING SHORT

Psalm 26:6 I will wash mine hands in innocency: so will I compass thine altar, O Lord.

I've failed You so many times, Lord. I have to hang my head in shame. I don't even know if You want me anymore. Forgive me. No excuses, Lord. Just, forgive me.

Lord, I feel so unworthy to come into Your presence. Forgive me for falling short of Your wonderful love.

Come now, and let us reason together,
saith the Lord:
though your sins be as scarlet,
they shall be as white as snow;
though they be red like crimson,
they shall be as wool.

By the loving gift of Your Son dying in my place, I have the privilege to come into Your presence freely.

I will heal their backsliding,
I will love them freely.

I can always escape to Your presence. You will teach me more and more that You are where I need to go for the peace and rest I need. Thank You for loving me and inviting me to spend time with You. Thank You for actually wanting me to spend time with You.

Isaiah 1:18   Hosea 14:4

FORGIVEN

Psalm 26:11 But as for me, I will walk in mine integrity: redeem me, and be merciful unto me.

What amazing love You have, Lord, that You would forgive me. Thank You, Jesus, for loving me enough to pay the penalty for my sins.

But God, who is rich in mercy,
for his great love wherewith he loved us,
even when we were dead in sins,
hath quickened us together with Christ,
(by grace ye are saved).

[T]he blood of Jesus Christ his Son cleanseth us
from all sin.

Thank You, Father, for sending Jesus to die for my sins so that I can be forgiven and washed clean from all the filth of my life.

Now ye are clean
through the word
which I [Jesus] have spoken unto you.

Thank You for giving me a new start, Lord. It feels so good to be clean and forgiven, so that I can come into Your presence and know that You will welcome me with open, loving arms. Thank You, Lord.

A new heart also will I give you,
and a new spirit will I put within you:
and I will take away the stony heart out of your
flesh, and I will give you an heart of flesh.

Ephesians 2:4-5   1 John 1:7   John 15:3   Ezekiel 36:26

SICK OF CHEMO

Psalm 27:6 And now shall mine head be lifted up above mine enemies round about me: therefore will I offer in his tabernacle sacrifices of joy; I will sing, yea, I will sing praises unto the Lord.

Lord, it's too much effort even to lift my head up off this pillow. All these lousy side effects make me feel like I'm surrounded by enemies who want to CHOP my head off. What an appropriate name those doctors gave my type of chemo–C.H.O.P.

I don't feel like singing. I feel like giving up. HELP ME, LORD! The chemo, the PICC line,* the nausea, the despair, my hair! I want to give up. I don't even care anymore.

And he said unto me,
My grace is sufficient for thee:
for my strength is made perfect in weakness.

May I, like Paul, respond, *Most gladly therefore will I rather glory in my infirmities, that the power of Christ may rest upon me.* But how can I do that?

C.H.O.P.: Christ Holds Our Palms. Christ Helps Our Pain. Christ's Hope Offers Peace. Christ Hinders Overwhelming Panic. Christ Harvests Our Praise. Christ's Hope Only Prevails. Change my thinking, Lord.

Lord Jesus Christ, by Your grace and power and hope and help, my head will be lifted up above this enemy facing me. I believe that there will be a time when I can sing praise to Your name. Even though I may not feel like it right now, I know that one day I will sing praise to Your name again.

* Peripherally inserted central catheter.

2 Corinthians 12:9

GRUMBLING AND COMPLAINING

Psalm 39:1 I said, I will take heed to my ways, that I sin not with my tongue: I will keep my mouth with a bridle, while the wicked is before me.

Spouting off and complaining and whining and cursing sure don't make things any easier. Sometimes I think my greatest enemy is my tongue, Lord. Oh, why can't I keep my mouth shut?

By Your grace, help me to pay attention to my attitude and actions. I never want to give a reason for the wicked ones to boast and rejoice because of something I've said.

Help me to remember: *Whoso keepeth his mouth and his tongue keepeth his soul from troubles. Proverbs 21:23*

I really want my tongue to be yielded to You.

I need You to do it through me.

Behold,
I am the Lord, the God of all flesh:
Is there any thing too hard for me?

For I the Lord thy God will hold thy right hand,
saying unto thee,
Fear not; I will help thee.

Jeremiah 32:27   Isaiah 41:13

FEELING THE WEIGHT OF SIN

Psalm 38:18 For I will declare mine iniquity; I will be sorry for my sin.

Lying here in bed has given me lots of time to think, Lord. I can't help but wonder how different things would be if I hadn't done certain things. I spend a lot of sleepless nights playing the game of "If Only." If only I hadn't done this. If only I hadn't done that. My mind is haunted with thoughts that it's my fault that I'm stuck here now. But there's nothing I can do about it.

Well, maybe there is something I can do. I can declare my iniquity–my sin–once and for all. Maybe I've asked Your forgiveness for everything before, maybe not. But today I come to You, Lord, and I admit that I've failed You. I admit I've sinned against You. I'm sorry for all that I've done–and all I haven't done. I ask You to forgive me for it all.

[H]e hath clothed me with the garments of salvation,
he hath covered me with the robe of righteousness,
as a bridegroom decketh himself with ornaments,
and as a bride adorneth herself with her jewels.

When thoughts of my sins come back to me, help me to remember that Your death on the cross covered all my sins. Help me to switch the focus from my sins to Your love. Thank You, Jesus, for loving me enough to pay the price for my sins. Help me to remember 1 Peter 1:18-19, which says, *Forasmuch as ye know that ye were not redeemed with corruptible things, as silver and gold...but with the precious blood of Christ, as of a lamb without blemish and without spot.*

Isaiah 61:10

FREED FROM THE WEIGHT OF SIN

Psalm 38:18 For I will declare mine iniquity; I will be sorry for my sin.

I can't believe that You paid the penalty for all my sins. There must be something I have to do—something I can do—to cover for my sins. It breaks my heart to think that You paid for all the wretched things I've done. I mean, You are God. You are pure. You are holy. And yet You took my sin on Yourself so that I might be forgiven. What awesome love!

If we confess our sins,
he is faithful and just to forgive us our sins,
and to cleanse us from all unrighteousness.

For when we were yet without strength,
in due time Christ died for the ungodly.
For scarcely for a righteous man will one die:
yet peradventure for a good man some would even
dare to die.
But God commendeth his love toward us, in that,
while we were yet sinners, Christ died for us.

Greater love hath no man than this,
that a man lay down his life for his friends.

Thank You, Jesus.

Romans 5:6-8   John 15:13   1 John 1:9   Isaiah 1:18

TO THE END OF LIFE

Psalm 30:12 To the end that my glory may sing praise to thee, and not be silent. O Lord my God, I will give thanks unto thee for ever.

"To the end." Those words just jump out at me; it doesn't matter what the verse really means. Those are such scary words to me.

I want to glorify You to the end of my life. I want to sing praise to You, even if my days are numbered. I want to give thanks to You.

I want to, but it's just not in me today to sing or say thank you.

Thus saith the Lord,
The heaven is my throne, and the earth is my
footstool...
For all those things hath mine hand made,
and all those things have been, saith the Lord:
but to this man will I look,
even to him that is poor and of a contrite spirit,
and trembleth at my word.

But will I ever be free from this pain and misery, Lord?

For, behold,
I [will] create new heavens and a new earth:
and the former shall not be remembered,
nor come into mind.
But be ye glad and rejoice for ever in that
which I create.

To the end? I guess there really never will be an end to my life, will there? Just an end to pain and suffering here. I believe–help my unbelief!

Isaiah 66:1-2   Isaiah 65:17-18

WHERE HAVE ALL THE SWEET THINGS GONE?

Psalm 104:33-34 I will sing unto the Lord as long as I live: I will sing praise to my God while I have my being. My meditation of him shall be sweet: I will be glad in the Lord.

Sweetness. It has been a long time since there has been much sweetness in my life.

There's no sweetness or comfort in my bed; no matter what position I am in, it's not comfortable.

There's no sweetness in listening to music; the sounds vibrate horribly through my body.

There is no sweetness in food; nothing tastes right. There's no sweetness in my mouth; chalky or metallic tastes from the meds change everything.

There's not much I can do about these things, Lord. But is it possible that my mind could be sweet? You know the battles that rage in my mind as I try to reconcile what Your Word says with what I am experiencing. Maybe I'll never have an answer here on earth, but can I trust You anyway?

> *O taste and see that the Lord is good:*
> *blessed is the man that trusteth in him.*

Sweeten my thinking, Lord. Give me hope to trust, to believe.

> *More to be desired are they [God's words] than gold,*
> *yea, than much fine gold:*
> *sweeter also than honey and the honeycomb.*

Is one way to sweeten my thinking by focusing on how sweet Your Word is, Lord?

Psalm 34:8   Psalm 19:10

GOD-CENTERED OR ME-CENTERED?

Psalm 145:1-2 I will extol thee, my God, O king; and I will bless thy name for ever and ever. Every day will I bless thee; and I will praise thy name for ever and ever.

From the moment I wake up in the morning, it seems all I do is focused on me.

I hate it when my world revolves around me. I get so caught up in making sure I take the right meds at the right time, making sure I do this and don't do that, watching this thing and watching that thing that may affect my health–I guess it's easy to make excuses for being so wrapped up in myself.

Like as a father pitieth his children,
so the Lord pitieth them that fear him.
For he knoweth our frame;
he remembereth that we are dust.

I am so glad You understand, Lord, but that's not the life I want to lead. I want my life to be God-centered, not cancer-centered or me-centered.

If I turn my attention to You and look for things to praise You for each day, then maybe that will help me focus on You and not me.

But I am so very thankful that You understand.

Psalm 103:13-14

CHURCH PRIORITIES

Psalm 5:7 But as for me, I will come into thy house in the multitude of thy mercy: and in thy fear will I worship toward thy holy temple.

Lord, sometimes I just get so busy with everything going on, I forget to make spending time in Your Word a priority.

I'm glad that Your mercy is so generous that I can still come to You, knowing that I am forgiven through Jesus.

You know church has been a challenge for me lately. By Your mercy I will be in church as soon as I am able, for I long to worship with others.

If thou turn away thy foot from the sabbath,
from doing thy pleasure on my holy day;
and call the sabbath a delight, the holy of the
Lord, honourable;
and shalt honour him,
not doing thine own ways, nor finding thine
own pleasure,
nor speaking thine own words:
Then shalt thou delight thyself in the Lord; and
I will cause thee to ride upon the high places of
the earth...
for the mouth of the Lord hath spoken it.

Help me to overcome those things that hold me back. Help me to trust that Your grace and mercy are sufficient.

Help me to make the Lord's Day special for You even when I can't be in church.

Isaiah 58:13-14

ENCOURAGING OTHERS

Psalm 34:11 Come, ye children, hearken unto me: I will teach You the fear of the Lord.

Lord, I've learned so much about You through all this. I sure wish I had known You better before, though, because the journey would have been easier.

[Jesus said,]
The Spirit of the Lord is upon me,
because he hath anointed me
to preach the gospel to the poor;
he hath sent me to heal the brokenhearted,
to preach deliverance to the captives,
and recovering of sight to the blind,
to set at liberty them that are bruised.

If You give me the opportunity, Lord, I want to help others learn some of what You have taught me. I want to help others learn what it means to fear the Lord and to feel a deep reverence and awe for You. I want others to learn what it is like to feel Your wonderful love and Your amazing peace and to know the incredible strength that can only come from You.

For whom he [God] did foreknow, he also
did predestinate
to be conformed to the image of his Son,
that he might be the firstborn among many brethren.

Help me to be like You, Lord. Help me to help others.

Luke 4:18   Romans 8:29

VICTORY THROUGH GOD

Psalm 44:5-6, 8 Through thee will we push down our enemies: through thy name will we tread them under that rise up against us. For I will not trust in my bow, neither shall my sword save me... In God we boast all the day long, and praise thy name forever.

God, it's got to be through You that I get victory. I can't do this on my own. I can't trust my own strength or my own wisdom or power.

It has to be through You that I get the victory over the evil cancer wreaking havoc in my body and attempting to destroy my soul.

It has to be through You that I get the victory over the despair that creeps into my soul.

Through You. I'm counting on You.

I have no other hope.

> *Thus saith the Lord the King of Israel,*
> *and his redeemer the Lord of hosts;*
> *I am the first, and I am the last;*
> *and beside me there is no God.*
> *Fear ye not, neither be afraid...*
>
> *Behold, I will do a new thing;*
> *now it shall spring forth; shall ye not know it?*
> *I will even make a way in the wilderness,*
> *and rivers in the desert.*

Isaiah 44:6, 8   Isaiah 43:19

I AM FEARFULLY AND
WONDERFULLY MADE

Psalm 139:14 I will praise thee; for I am fearfully and wonderfully made: marvellous are thy works; and that my soul knoweth right well.

Lord, the human body is a marvelous, incredible creation. It is mind-boggling how well our bodies function.

I praise You for Your work in designing us so perfectly. I ask You to work within my body to help it to function properly.

Thus saith the Lord, thy redeemer,
and he that formed thee from the womb,
I am the Lord that maketh all things;
that stretcheth forth the heavens alone;
that spreadeth abroad the earth by myself;

Even every one that is called by my name:
for I have created him for my glory,
I have formed him;
yea, I have made him.

I praise You, Father, for the marvels of the human body. In Your mercy and wisdom, help my immune system to function just as You originally designed it–to rid this body of the cancer and toxins.

Isaiah 44:24   Isaiah 43:7

CALL ON THE LORD

Psalm 55:16 As for me, I will call upon God; and the Lord shall save me.

I will call upon You, Lord. You are my strength and my salvation.

Other people may fail me. Others may disappoint me. Others may even break my heart with their insensitivity and their uncaring ways.

But as for me, I will call upon You, because I know You are the One who will never let me down. You will never fail me.

For I am the Lord,
I change not.

Call unto me,
and I will answer thee,
and shew thee great and mighty things,
which thou knowest not.

I believe that.

Help my unbelief.

Malachi 3:6   Jeremiah 33:3

WHEN DOCTORS FAIL

Psalm 55:23 But thou, O God... I will trust in thee.

The doctors blew it, Lord. How can I trust them now?

But You allowed it. How can I trust You?

But if I don't have You to trust, I have nothing.

If I were God, I certainly wouldn't allow this kind of thing to happen to one of my children. Why do You?

But who am I to question You? Can I balance a single star in space? Can I create life out of nothing? Can I create a single flower? Can I cause the sun to rise or to stop rising? Can I stop the tides?

No. So, as hard as it is for me to understand, I acknowledge that You are sovereign and that You love me.

I can only cling to You with the words of Job: *Though he slay me, yet will I trust in him. Job 13:15*

In all their affliction he was afflicted,
and the angel of his presence saved them:
in his love and in his pity he redeemed them;
and he bare them,
and carried them all the days of old.

[Jesus said,]
I will not leave you comfortless:
I will come to you.

Isaiah 63:9   John 14:18

FEAR

Psalm 56:3 What time I am afraid, I will trust in thee.

Fear creeps in so quietly in the dead of night. I think I'm not afraid, but then my heart gets squeezed in the vise of fear, and I feel powerless to do anything.

Then I remember Your Word. I don't have to be held captive by fear when I choose to trust in You.

The Lord is my light and my salvation; whom shall
I fear?
the Lord is the strength of my life; of whom shall I be
afraid?

Behold, God is my salvation; I will trust, and not be
afraid:
for the Lord Jehovah is my strength and my song;
he also is become my salvation.

For God hath not given us the spirit of fear;
but of power, and of love, and of a sound mind.

Sometimes I don't feel like You are very trustworthy, but that's because I can see only a tiny part of the picture. You see it all. You know that through this challenge You can and You will work things out for good.

And so I will trust in You, Lord. I may have to remind myself to trust You a thousand times a day, but still I will trust in You.

I choose to trust You. Please keep the fear away.

Psalm 27:1   Isaiah 12:2   2 Timothy 1:7

FAILING FLESH

Psalm 56:4 In God I will praise his word, in God I have put my trust; I will not fear what flesh can do unto me.

My flesh is tearing me apart, Lord. The pain, the nausea, the headaches, the sores, the agony—the list is endless.
I think, "How much more of this can I take?"
But then I remember that Paul said in 2 Corinthians 4:16: *For which cause we faint not; but though our outward man perish, yet the inward man is renewed day by day.*
Renew me, Lord.
Renew my trust in You. Renew my ability to praise You. Renew my heart.
Renew hope.

> *Hearken unto me, O [children of God]...*
> *which were borne by me from the belly,*
> *which are carried from the womb:*
> *And even to your old age I am he;*
> *and even to [gray] hairs will I carry you:*
> *I have made,*
> *and I will bear;*
> *even I will carry,*
> *and will deliver you.*

Isaiah 46:3-4

ARE YOU LISTENING, LORD?

Psalm 57:2 I will cry unto God most high; unto God that performeth all things for me.

God! Can't You hear me crying out to You?
Why don't You answer me?
Where have You gone?

> *The eyes of the Lord are upon the righteous,*
> *and his ears are open unto their cry.*

Don't You care?

> *[Cast] all your care upon him;*
> *for he careth for you.*

Help me to believe that You care and that with Your help, everything will work out for me.

> *For thus saith the high and lofty One that*
> *inhabiteth eternity,*
> *whose name is Holy;*
> *I dwell in the high and holy place,*
> *with him also that is of a contrite and humble spirit,*
> *to revive the spirit of the humble,*
> *and to revive the heart of the contrite ones.*

Psalm 34:15   1 Peter 5:7   Isaiah 57:15

FIX MY HEART

Psalm 57:7 My heart is fixed, O God, my heart is fixed: I will sing and give praise.

Huh! If my heart were fixed, it wouldn't have this big, gaping hole in it!

I know that's not what the verse means, Lord, but I hurt so much! I know that "fixed" in this verse means that I'm resting in you, but how can I? When I read this verse the word "fixed" just jumps out at me, because my heart is not fixed. My heart is tattered and scarred from memories that haunt me.

Why do I have to go through this alone? Why do these memories have to slash at my heart and stab at my conscience, breaking my heart again and again?

And I will give them one heart,
and one way,
that they may fear me for ever,
for the good of them,
and of their children after them.

Fix my heart, Lord. I can't fix it myself.
Fix my broken, bleeding heart.

But we all,
with open face beholding as in a glass
the glory of the Lord,
are changed into the same image
from glory to glory,
even as by the Spirit of the Lord.

Jeremiah 32:39   2 Corinthians 3:18

SING TO THE LORD

Psalm 57:9 I will praise thee, O Lord, among the people: I will sing unto thee among the nations.

Yes, Lord, I will sing. It doesn't matter to You whether I have the most beautiful voice or whether my songs sound like the scraping of a fingernail on a chalkboard.

Today I am alive, and I will sing to You.

I cannot tell what tomorrow holds, but with the wisps of hope holding me up, I will sing to You today.

> *And he hath put a new song in my mouth,*
> *even praise unto our God:*
> *many shall see it, and fear,*
> *and shall trust in the Lord.*

> *Let the word of Christ dwell in you richly*
> *in all wisdom;*
> *teaching and admonishing one another*
> *in psalms and hymns and spiritual songs,*
> *singing with grace in your hearts to the Lord.*

What song would You like me to sing, Lord?

Psalm 40:3   Colossians 3:16

THROUGH ANOTHER DAY

Psalm 59:16 But I will sing of thy power; yea, I will sing aloud of thy mercy in the morning: for thou hast been my defence and refuge in the day of my trouble.

You got me through again, Lord. I wasn't sure I'd make it, but here I am with another day to praise You.

Shelter me, Lord. Just let me rest in You for a while before the next battle begins.

> *[God is] a strength to the poor,*
> *a strength to the needy in his distress,*
> *a refuge from the storm,*
> *a shadow from the heat,*
> *when the blast of the terrible ones*
> *is as a storm against the wall.*

Truly, You are my refuge. My fortress. My protection in this raging battle for life. I know I won't win all the battles. But I know Who has already won the war. I believe Your Word which says in Romans 8:35-39:

> *Who shall separate us from the love of Christ? Shall tribulation, or distress, or persecution, or famine, or nakedness, or peril, or sword? As it is written, For thy sake we are killed all the day long; we are accounted as sheep for the slaughter.*
>
> *Nay, in all these things we are more than conquerors through him that loved us.*
>
> *For I am persuaded, that neither death, nor life, nor angels, nor principalities, nor powers, nor things present, nor things to come, nor height, nor depth, nor any other creature, shall be able to separate us*

from the love of God, which is in Christ Jesus our Lord.

Isaiah 25:4

GUT-WRENCHING CRIES

Psalm 119:145 I cried with my whole heart; hear me,
O Lord: I will keep thy statutes.

I never knew I could cry such deep, gut-wrenching cries.
I feel like a wrung-out dishrag when I am through.

I certainly can relate to David when he said, *I am weary
with my groaning; all the night make I my bed to swim; I
water my couch with my tears. Psalm 6:6*

> *[God] shall deliver the needy when he crieth;*
> *the poor also, and him that hath no helper.*
> *He shall spare the poor and needy,*
> *and shall save the souls of the needy.*

*Hear my prayer, O Lord, and give ear unto my cry;
hold not thy peace at my tears: for I am a stranger
with thee . . . O spare me, that I may recover strength,
before I go hence, and be no more. Psalm 39:12-13*

> *God shall wipe away all tears from their eyes;*
> *and there shall be no more death,*
> *neither sorrow,*
> *nor crying,*
> *neither shall there be any more pain:*
> *for the former things are passed away.*

How I look forward to that time in eternity!
Help me to hang on, Lord. Dry my tears.

Psalm 72:12-13   Revelations 21:4

I'VE FAILED

Psalm 32:5 I acknowledged my sin unto thee, and mine iniquity have I not hid. I said, I will confess my transgressions unto the Lord; and thou forgavest the iniquity of my sin. Selah.

Auuugggghhhhhh. I did it again, Lord. I wish I wouldn't do that! I wish I were perfect.

But I guess it does no good to wish.

Forgive me, Lord.

There's no use trying to hide what I've done. I confess to You that I did just the thing that I knew would disappoint You. Now, I'm so sorry. So very sorry, Lord.

For thus saith the Lord God, the Holy One of Israel;
In returning and rest shall ye be saved;
in quietness and in confidence shall be your
strength...
And therefore will the Lord wait, that he may be
gracious unto you,
and therefore will he be exalted,
that he may have mercy upon you:
for the Lord is a God of judgment:
blessed are all they that wait for him.

How thankful I am that You forgave me in the past, that You forgive me today, and that You will forgive me tomorrow.

Thank You, Jesus, for paying the penalty for my sin. It breaks my heart to think about how You suffered because of my sins. But thank You for forgiving me.

Isaiah 30:15, 18

CAN'T SLEEP

Psalm 119:62 At midnight I will rise to give thanks unto thee because of thy righteous judgments.

Ten o'clock.
Eleven o'clock.
Midnight.
One o'clock.
Two o'clock.

Why do I even bother going to bed? I can't sleep. I wonder what it was that kept the author of Psalm 119 awake?

Maybe I should just do what the psalmist said in Psalm 119:62: *At midnight I will rise to give thanks to You.*

Enter into his gates with thanksgiving
and into his courts with praise:
be thankful unto him,
and bless his name.

Tonight, if I can't sleep, I will start counting things I can thank You for, Lord. If I have to, I'll start going through the alphabet to prompt my mind to think of things.

Acceptance– Thank You, Lord, for accepting me as I am.

Breath– Thank You, Lord, that I can breathe. It may hurt everywhere else, but at least it doesn't hurt to breathe.

Cats– Thank You, Lord, for my cat. He is such a comfort to me.

D . . .

Psalm 100:4

I AM LOVED BY GOD

Psalm 61:4 I will abide in thy tabernacle for ever: I will trust in the covert [cover or shelter] of thy wings. Selah.

That's about all I've got the strength to do today: to lie on this couch and feel Your loving presence with me.

It is such an amazing thought, my Friend. I can't do anything. I don't look very attractive. I've been puking my brains out. Right about now, there's nothing that would cause anyone to love me.

And yet You love me. You wrap me in Your gentle, cushioning love like a cozy down comforter wraps me in its airy warmth.

Today I will bask in the shelter and comfort of Christ's loving embrace. I need do no more than that.

Herein is love, not that we loved God,
but that he loved us,
and sent his Son to be the propitiation for our sins.

And we have known and believed
the love that God hath to us.
God is love;
and he that dwelleth in love dwelleth in God,
and God in him.

1 John 4:10   1 John 4:16

I AM LOVED BY GOD

Hereby perceive we the love of God, because he laid down his life for us.
1 John 3:16

But God, who is rich in mercy, for his great love wherewith he loved us, Even when we were dead in sins, hath quickened us together with Christ, (by grace ye are saved;) And hath raised us up together, and made us sit together in heavenly places in Christ Jesus: That in the ages to come he might shew the exceeding riches of his grace in his kindness toward us through Christ Jesus. For by grace are ye saved through faith; and that not of yourselves: it is the gift of God.
Ephesians 2:4-8

For we ourselves also were sometimes foolish, disobedient, deceived, serving divers lusts and plea-sures, living in malice and envy, hateful, and hating one another. But after that the kindness and love of God our Saviour toward man appeared, Not by works of righteousness which we have done, but according to his mercy he saved us.
Titus 3:3-5

And the grace of our Lord was exceeding abundant with faith and love which is in Christ Jesus.
1 Timothy 1:14

The Lord hath appeared of old unto me, saying, Yea, I have loved thee with an everlasting love: therefore with lovingkindness have I drawn thee.
Jeremiah 31:3

TELLING OTHERS

Psalm 66:16 Come and hear, all ye that fear God, and
I will declare what he hath done for my soul.

Lord, You've helped me. You've strengthened me.
You've forgiven me when I lashed out at You. You've given
me hope when it seemed there was nothing to hope for. In
mercy, You've wrapped me in Your arms of love.

I couldn't go through this adversity without You.

But I wonder about all those others who don't know You?
How do they survive?

It must be so lonely and scary not to have You to hold
their hand when they go through the valley of the shadow of
death.

Isn't there something I can do? Some way I can help
them?

Jesus . . . saith unto him,
Go home to thy friends, and
tell them how great things the Lord hath
done for thee,
and hath had compassion on thee.

I want to help others by sharing stories with them about
what You have done for me.

Please give me opportunities to tell others about Your
wonderful works. Lead me to someone who is open to hear
about Your love and mercy and hope and strength.

Mark 5:19

UNSATISFIED

Psalm 69:30 I will praise the name of God with a song, and will magnify him with thanksgiving.

Why am I so unsatisfied? I need You to change my focus, Lord.

[W]hatsoever things are true,
whatsoever things are honest,
whatsoever things are just,
whatsoever things are pure,
whatsoever things are lovely,
whatsoever things are of good report;
if there be any virtue, and
if there be any praise,
think on these things.

Of course. It makes perfect sense. It's no wonder that I keep thinking about all the negative things, all the bad things, all the depressing things. It's because that's all there is in my life right now–bad, depressing, and negative news. At least, it feels that way.

It is of the Lord's mercies that we are not consumed,
because his compassions fail not.
They are new every morning:
great is thy faithfulness.
The LORD is my portion, saith my soul;
therefore will I hope in him.
The Lord is good unto them that wait for him,
to the soul that seeketh him.

Open my eyes to see the good things around me. Forgive me for grumbling and complaining. Forgive me for always thinking the worst. Enable me to see the things You want me to see–positive things and not negative things.

Philippians 4:8   Lamentations 3:22-25

IS THERE ANY HOPE?

Psalm 71:14 But I will hope continually, and will yet praise thee more and more.

Hope?
Who has hope? Not me. It's been so long, I think I've even forgotten what hope is.

I don't want to stay in the clutches of hopelessness, God. There's certainly no joy and no peace in my heart when hopelessness reigns there. But I'm afraid there's nothing left to hope for, God. Nothing.

Now the God of hope
fill you with all joy and peace in believing,
that ye may abound in hope,
through the power of the Holy Ghost.

So I ask You, God of Hope, to fill me with joy and peace— help me to believe Your promises. May I abound in hope through the power of the Holy Spirit. Fill me, infuse me with divine hope. Please.

Romans 15:13

UNDER THE KNIFE

Psalm 56:11 In God have I put my trust: I will not be afraid what man can do unto me.

Under the knife again. Lord, You know how hard this is for me. I am frightened when I think of all the things that could go wrong. Do You know how many people die each year from mistakes doctors make? Why must I go through this again?

The fear of man bringeth a snare:
but whoso putteth his trust in the Lord shall be safe.

I am caught up in that snare, Lord. My fear of what could happen holds me captive; I can't get this out of my mind, and I have no peace.

I guess I do have a choice, though, Lord. I can choose to fear the mistakes people might make, or I can choose to trust You. God, I cry out to You! Help me to trust You! Help me to believe that You will keep me safe. Help me to believe that whatever happens, You will be with me, helping me, strengthening me.

As an act of my will, I put my trust in You. *What time I am afraid, I will trust in You* (Psalm 56:3). I ask You to work through each of the doctors, technicians, and nurses. May it be Your hand that performs the surgery and guides my follow-up care. By Your grace, I have put my trust in You.

[The Lord] hath said,
I will never leave thee, nor forsake thee.
So that we may boldly say,
The Lord is my helper,
and I will not fear what man shall do unto me.

Proverbs 29:25   Hebrews 13:5-6

WHEN I'M WEAK

Psalm 71:16 I will go in the strength of the Lord God: I will make mention of thy righteousness, even of thine only.

Not again.

I can't face this day again. I can't do it. It was easier in the beginning when I didn't know what was going to happen. But now I know, and my stomach churns at the thought.

The only way I can put another foot forward toward the next chemo treatment is with Your strength. *My flesh and my heart faileth: but God is the strength of my heart.* Psalm 73:26

> *Hast thou not known? hast thou not heard,*
> *that the everlasting God, the Lord,*
> *the Creator of the ends of the earth,*
> *fainteth not, neither is weary?*
> *there is no searching of his understanding.*
> *He giveth power to the faint;*
> *and to them that have no might he*
> *increaseth strength.*
> *Even the youths shall faint and be weary,*
> *and the young men shall utterly fall:*
> *But they that wait upon the Lord shall*
> *renew their strength;*
> *they shall mount up with wings as eagles;*
> *they shall run, and not be weary;*
> *and they shall walk, and not faint.*

I will go in the strength of the Lord. I am not going through this alone. I will go in Your strength. I will meditate on Your Word, which reminds me that You are the source of my strength.

Isaiah 40:28-31

GODLY MUSIC

Psalm 71:22 I will also praise thee with the psaltery, even thy truth, O my God: unto thee will I sing with the harp, O thou Holy One of Israel.

Music. Why didn't I think of this sooner? Music soothes my aching soul and brings comfort to me. I think of Paul and Silas when they were in prison in the dead of night, and they were singing praises to You. They'd been beaten and tortured; their bodies were bloody and raw. Yet they were singing praises to You.

And the multitude rose up together against them: and the magistrates rent off their clothes, and commanded to beat them. And when they had laid many stripes upon them, they cast them into prison, charging the jailer to keep them safely: Who ...thrust them into the inner prison, and made their feet fast in the stocks. And at midnight Paul and Silas prayed, and sang praises unto God: and the prisoners heard them.

I used to think that Paul and Silas must have been some type of Super Christians to be able to do that. But then I learned. Godly music is God's EMLA cream that helps to take some of the pain away. When I worship You by listening to godly music, my soul and spirit are transported to a realm where I am not shackled by the physical body.

He brought me up also out of an horrible pit, out of the miry clay, and set my feet upon a rock, and estab-lished my goings. And he hath put a new song in my mouth, even praise unto our God: many shall see it, and fear, and shall trust in the Lord.

When my body cries out in pain, may it be a reminder to step outside this physical realm into Your presence through true worship.

Acts 16:22-25   Psalm 40:2-3

DESPITE CANCER

Psalm 77:10-11 And I said, This is my infirmity: but I will remember the years of the right hand of the most High. I will remember the works of the Lord: surely I will remember thy wonders of old.

Okay, so I've got cancer. I don't have to let it consume my whole life. I can choose what I will think about during all those long, quiet times: waiting, driving to or from treatment, being so sick I can't do anything, and all those long hours of sleeplessness.

I can choose where I let my mind wander, and I can choose to let it dwell on You.

For the weapons of our warfare are not carnal,
but mighty through God to the pulling down of
strong holds;
Casting down imaginations, and every high thing
that exalteth itself against the knowledge of God,
and bringing into captivity every thought to the
obedience of Christ.

Bring back to my mind, Lord, those stories in the Bible where You performed "wonders of old."

Help me to see those times in my past where You were working in my life. Help me to remember all the prayers You have answered.

Guide my thoughts to think what You would want me to think.

2 Corinthians 10:4-5

FORGOTTEN BLESSINGS

Psalm 77:12 I will meditate also of all thy work, and talk of thy doings.

I can't concentrate on anything for more than two minutes. So how can I meditate on anything?

I know You are answering prayer. I know You're doing things. But my mind draws a blank when I try to think of the things You have done for me and my family.

My problems are so huge, they seem to overshadow Your blessings. I can relate to Jeremiah in Lamentations 3:18-25: *And I said, my strength and my hope is perished from the Lord: Remembering mine affliction and my misery, the wormwood and the gall. My soul hath them still in remembrance, and is humbled in me.*

I guess I should focus more on the rest of that passage when Jeremiah said, *This I recall to my mind, therefore have I hope. It is of the Lord's mercies that we are not consumed, because his compassions fail not. They are new every morning: great is thy faithfulness. The Lord is my portion, saith my soul; therefore will I hope in him. The Lord is good unto them that wait for him, to the soul that seeketh him.*

You have been good to me, Lord, so I know what I'll do. I'll start writing down some of the things I see You doing in my life and in other people's lives. That way I'll be sure to remember them and be encouraged by Your faithfulness.

Open my eyes to be able to see all the things You are doing in my life, and I will write each one down. At least I'll try.

HEARING GOD

Psalm 85:8 I will hear what God the Lord will speak: for he will speak peace unto his people, and to his saints.

Lord, I'm listening. I can't do much else right about now. I need to hear from You. I need Your voice to speak peace to my heart.

> *Thou [God] wilt keep him in perfect peace,*
> *whose mind is stayed on thee:*
> *because he trusteth in thee.*

Help me always to listen for Your voice and not to turn aside and trust other foolish voices.

> *Be still,*
> *and know that I am God:*
> *I will be exalted among the heathen,*
> *I will be exalted in the earth.*

Thank You, Lord, for Your peace.

Isaiah 26:3   Psalm 46:10

HELP ME!

Psalm 86:7 In the day of my trouble I will call upon thee: for thou wilt answer me.

God, I'm holding You to Your word. You said that if I called on You in the day of my trouble, You would answer me.
HELP!!!!!!!!
Answer me, Lord! Help me know what I should do.
Help me to keep on going. Help me not to give up.
Help me not to believe the lies in my mind that You don't love me. Help me not to believe the lies in my mind that You don't care.
Help me!
You said You would...

For the word of the Lord is right;
and all his works are done in truth.

The Lord upholdeth all that fall,
and raiseth up all those that be bowed down.

For the Lord loveth judgment,
and forsaketh not his saints;
they are preserved for ever.

Psalm 33:4   Psalm 145:14   Psalm 37:28

THE SHADOW OF DEATH

Psalm 23:4 Yea, though I walk through the valley of the shadow of death, I will fear no evil: for thou art with me; thy rod and thy staff they comfort me.

Help.

Help me, Lord.

Hold me up.

> *For I the Lord thy God*
> *will hold thy right hand,*
> *saying unto thee,*
> *Fear not;*
> *I will help thee.*
>
> *I will never leave thee,*
> *nor forsake thee.*

Isaiah 41:13   Hebrews 13:5

TEACH ME YOUR WAYS

Psalm 86:11 Teach me thy way, O Lord; I will walk
in thy truth: unite my heart to fear thy name.

Lord, teach me Your way. I've tried my own way, and it
hasn't worked very well. I think I am so smart and that I can
figure things out on my own. But my own way has led only
to heartache and misery with no hope.

I want to learn Your way; I want to be willing to walk in
Your truth. What can I do to retrain my thinking?

*Come unto me, all ye that labour and are heavy
laden, and I will give you rest.*

*Take my yoke upon you, and learn of me;
for I am meek and lowly in heart:
and ye shall find rest unto your souls.
For my yoke is easy,
and my burden is light.*

*I will instruct thee
and teach thee
in the way which thou shalt go:
I will guide thee with mine eye.*

Matthew 11:28-30   Psalm 32:8

FIGHTING FOR MY FAMILY

Psalm 45:17 I will make thy name to be remembered in all generations: therefore shall the people praise thee for ever and ever.

Lord, help me remember that I'm not fighting just for myself. I'm fighting for my family. I'm fighting so I can be a part of my children's and my grandchildren's lives.

But if You choose a different path for my future than I would have chosen, help me to be content with Your will.

Help me to live out the rest of my life in such a way that my family and others will praise You.

Thus saith the Lord that made thee,
and formed thee from the womb,
which will help thee;
Fear not, O Jacob, my servant...
whom I have chosen.

For I will pour water upon him that is thirsty,
and floods upon the dry ground:
I will pour my spirit upon thy seed,
and my blessing upon thine offspring.

May my suffering not be worthless; may it accomplish Your will for eternity.

Isaiah 44:2-3

A GOOD DAY

Psalm 86:12 I will praise thee, O Lord my God, with all my heart: and I will glorify thy name for evermore.

Ah! It feels so good to wake up and actually feel human, Lord! I can see the sky is blue today, but today it wouldn't even matter if it was gray!

It has been so long since I awoke feeling like my old self. Could this be true, bubbly happiness I am feeling?

It's amazing, Lord, because I was beginning to think I would never be happy again. Truly, You are a great God, and You have worked in Your wondrous ways to help me to feel well today.

Behold, we count them happy which endure.
Ye have heard of the patience of Job,
and have seen the end of the Lord;
that the Lord is very pitiful, and of tender mercy.

I praise You, O Lord my God, for today.

I don't know how I will feel tomorrow. But today I feel great, and I want to praise You with all my heart for this one simple day of bubbly happiness.

James 5:11

ARE YOU REALLY FAITHFUL, GOD?

Psalm 89:1 I will sing of the mercies of the Lord for ever: with my mouth will I make known thy faithfulness to all generations.

With my mouth I'll make known Your faithfulness? Hah! Everything in my mouth tastes horrible–including the taste of Your faithfulness.

How can You say You have been faithful to me? How can You let me suffer and say You are faithful? I don't see it. I don't feel it. I don't want it!

What happened to the lovingkindness You promised me? What happened to the goodness of the Lord? What about Jesus's words in Matthew 11:28: *"Come unto me, all ye that labour and are heavy laden, and I will give you rest"?*
Where is that rest? I'm exhausted, and I don't understand what You are doing.

I'm sorry. I just can't praise You today, Lord.

If we believe not,

yet he abideth faithful:

he cannot deny himself.

2 Timothy 2:13

CRUSHED

Psalm 92:4 For thou, Lord, hast made me glad through thy work: I will triumph in the works of thy hands.

I got a bouquet of flowers from my friend's garden today. When I was alone, I took one of the wild roses and breathed deeply its rich perfume. But then the thorn pricked my finger. My serene vision of being in a field of fragrant flowers was shattered, and I was back in the realm of pokes and prods and sterile smells.

I couldn't help myself; I ripped that rose to shreds. Where did that burst of anger come from, Lord?

I had to clean up the mess before anyone saw it. Piece by piece, I picked up the pulverized petals and piled them in my hand. It was then that I noticed the scent again. It was stronger than when I had first breathed in the flower's fragrance. It made me cry.

Lord, I hate this anger I have! I feel like I'm being crushed by everything that's happening in my life, and I lash out. But I want to be like that flower. In the midst of this crushing, I want the fragrance of Your peace and hope in me to be like a perfume to those around me.

Beloved, now are we the sons of God,
and it doth not yet appear what we shall be:
but we know that, when he shall appear,
we shall be like him; for we shall see him as he is.

Now the God of peace ... make you perfect ...
working in you that which is wellpleasing in
his sight, through Jesus Christ; to whom be
glory for ever and ever.

I ask that You would grant me the fragrance of Your peace, so that I won't be a thorn-poke to those around me.

1 John 3:2   Hebrews 13:20-21

MY REFUGE

Psalm 91:2 I will say of the Lord, He is my refuge and my fortress: my God; in him will I trust.

"I will say of the Lord, He is my refuge and my fortress." Oh, how very true those words are, my Forever-Friend. There is no way I could go through this without You. There is no way I would want to go through this without You.

I am so thankful for family and friends, but the comfort they give doesn't reach down into the deepest depths of my soul. You alone can give that kind of comfort.

The beloved of the Lord shall dwell in safety by him;
and the Lord shall cover him all the day long,
and he shall dwell between his shoulders.

Lord, that verse makes it sound like You're giving me a big hug, keeping me close to You. Whether I am frightened or furious; worried or wiped out; jealous or just plain bitter; I can hide in You. I can bring all my thoughts and questions to You, and You listen. In the end, I find myself weeping on Your shoulder, wrapped in the everlasting arms of Your merciful love. Or I find myself refreshed and energized by Your presence as I ask for Your forgiveness for my lack of faith.

The eternal God is thy refuge,
and underneath are the everlasting arms.

For he knoweth our frame;
he remembereth that we are dust.

Thank You for being my refuge and my fortress, where I can take shelter in the midst of this storm. Thank You for the safety I find in You. Thank You for forgiving me, holding me tight, and telling me again and again that You love me. Regardless.

Deuteronomy 33:12   Deuteronomy 33:27   Psalm 103:14

I WILL LIVE AND NOT DIE

Psalm 116:9 I will walk before the Lord in the land of the living.

I believe that I will live and not die.

I will not give up or give in to the enemy within. By Your power and strength, Lord, I will rise from this bed, and I will walk in the "Land of the Living."

And if for some reason You choose to take me home to heaven before I walk in the "Land of the Living" here on earth, I know that I will walk in the Eternal Land of the Living. Though my body may die, my soul will live forever, and I will walk with You in Heaven.

Jesus said unto her,
I am the resurrection, and the life:
he that believeth in me, though he were dead,
yet shall he live:
And whosoever liveth and believeth
in me shall never die.
Believest thou this?

One way or another, I will walk before You in the Land of the Living.

Cancer will not win.

John 11:25-26

FOREVER

Psalm 75:9 But I will declare for ever; I will sing praises to the God of Jacob.

All I see, day after day, are the four walls around me. I forget that anything else exists. It's just me and my aches and my pains and my despair. That's it.

But then the dark clouds of despair part, and I get a glimpse of something more: a glimpse of eternity.

There is so much more to life than what I am experiencing here and now. My body may be in danger of dying, but I am not my body. I am spirit and soul, living in this body temporarily. I, the real me, will live on forever–regardless of what may happen to this flesh and bones.

[Jesus said,] In my Father's house are many
mansions...
I go to prepare a place for you.
And if I go and prepare a place for you,
I will come again, and receive you unto myself;
that where I am, there ye may be also.

As it is written,
Eye hath not seen, nor ear heard,
neither have entered into the heart of man,
the things which God hath prepared
for them that love him.

Give me vision, Lord, to see beyond what my physical eyes can see. Turn my heart toward eternity. Not because I could die, but because I am alive! I will never die!

Set me free from the shackles of depression and despair.

John 14:2-3   1 Corinthians 2:9

LONGING FOR CROWDS

Psalm 35:18 I will give thee thanks in the great congregation: I will praise thee among much people.

Wouldn't that be nice. To praise You in the great congregation. But right now I'm stuck here in the house, waiting for my white blood cell count to go up. I am so sick of this process. I am so lonely.

I want to be back out there among the crowds of people. I want to be able to praise You among many people. I want to be able to go to the mall without worrying if I'm going to bring home more than just full shopping bags.

Let your conversation be without covetousness;
and be content with such things as ye have:
for [Jesus] hath said,
I will never leave thee, nor forsake thee.

By faith I believe that I will be able to give You thanks in the great congregation. I will praise You among many people—even if it's silently praising You for being able to bump shoulders with people in the grocery store line.

Until that time, help me to be content with Your presence alone.

Hebrews 13:5

IN CONTROL

Psalm 119:15-16 I will meditate in thy precepts, and have respect unto thy ways. I will delight myself in thy statutes: I will not forget thy word.

Sometimes it feels like I have no control over anything that is going on around me. But I need to feel like I have some degree of control over my life. Is there anything I can control?

I guess this verse from Psalms gives me some ideas of what I can control. I can be in control of what I allow in my mind. I can choose to meditate on Your Word. I can choose to memorize verses that encourage me.

I can be in control of my attitude toward the Bible; I can choose to delight myself in Your Word. I can be in control of whether or not I will obey You, so I can choose to live a life that is pleasing to You.

When I look at it this way, I realize that I can have a lot of control over some really important things in my life. But the bottom line is, I can't even control these things, can I? I need You to work through me.

Blessed is the man that trusteth in the Lord,
and whose hope the Lord is.
For he shall be as a tree planted by the waters,
and that spreadeth out her roots by the river,
and shall not see when heat cometh,
but her leaf shall be green;
and shall not be careful in the year of drought,
neither shall cease from yielding fruit.

Jeremiah 17:7-8

OTHERS' LIES

Psalm 119:69 The proud have forged a lie against me:
but I will keep thy precepts with my whole heart.

I know people are talking about me. It drives me crazy to
think about what people are saying. Why do people have to
be so mean? What did I ever do to hurt them?

In three thousand years since that psalm was written, I
guess people haven't changed. They lied about the author of
Psalm 119, and they still lie today. Sometimes it makes me
want to spread lies about them, too. Then they'll know how
it feels!

Vengeance is mine;
I will repay, saith the Lord.

Okay, Lord. Help me to do what's right even if I don't
think some people deserve it. Help me to forgive others for the
evil they do to us. Help me to keep on loving You even when
others treat me unjustly. Help me not to hold it against You
for not protecting me in the way that I think You should.

For what glory is it,
if, when ye be buffeted for your faults,
ye shall take it patiently?
but if, when ye do well, and suffer for it,
ye take it patiently,
this is acceptable with God.

Lord, I need Your help: I want to choose to take the
higher road–Your road. Give me the strength to keep Your
ways with my whole heart–and not halfheartedly.

Romans 12:19   1 Peter 2:20

ROTTEN NURSE

Psalm 119:78 Let the proud be ashamed; for they dealt perversely with me without a cause: but I will meditate in thy precepts.

What is wrong with that nurse! I hate it when she is on duty. She always acts like she is such a know-it-all and doesn't even listen to a word I say. Why do they let her keep working here? I would have fired her months ago.

I don't know what her problem is, but she seems to have it in for me. It's almost as if she aggravates me on purpose. Sometimes it's all I can do to keep from kicking her–or at least tripping her when she walks by me.

That's not the right attitude, I know. I need to focus more on Your way of doing things, not my own fleshly way. So what precept or principle should I be thinking about when it comes to dealing with her?

Love your enemies, bless them that curse you,
do good to them that hate you,
and pray for them which despitefully use you.

Lord, I need You to love her through me. I don't know what she's going through in her own life. Make me a bright spot in her day. Use me to encourage her. May she see You in me.

Blessed are ye, when men shall revile you,
and persecute you, and shall say all manner of evil
against you falsely, for my sake.
Rejoice, and be exceeding glad:
for great is your reward in heaven.

Matthew 5:44   Matthew 5:11-12

93

A BETTER DAY

Psalm 119:93 I will never forget thy precepts: for with them thou hast quickened me.

It's amazing, Lord. When I start my day by spending time with You and reading the Bible, my whole day goes better. What is there about the Word of God that seems to give me life? It's like spiritual food for my soul.

Thank You for reviving my spirit, Lord.

It is the spirit that quickeneth; the flesh
profiteth nothing:
the words that I speak unto you,
they are spirit, and they are life.

Thank You for Your Word, which has so many wonderful promises to claim. I am amazed at the way You always have just what I need in Your Word.

The God of our Lord Jesus Christ, the Father of glory,...
give unto you the spirit of wisdom and revelation
in the knowledge of him:
The eyes of your understanding being enlightened;
that ye may know what is the hope of his calling,
and what the riches of the glory of his
inheritance in the saints.

Thank You for the Holy Spirit who helps me understand what I read in the Bible. What a difference there is when, before I read the Bible, I ask Your Holy Spirit to teach me and give me understanding. Thank You for giving me Your Spirit to be my Teacher.

John 6:63   Ephesians 1:17-18

VICTORY DAY

Psalm 30:1 I will extol thee, O Lord; for thou hast lifted me up, and hast not made my foes to rejoice over me.

You did it, Lord! I felt so absolutely miserable before, but You have lifted me up! You have helped me through that battle, and I praise You for it. The enemies of pain and despair did not win the battle, and they won't win the war.

> *Sing and rejoice, O daughter of Zion:*
> *for, lo, I come,*
> *and I will dwell in the midst of thee,*
> *saith the Lord.*

> *Behold,*
> *my servants shall sing for joy of heart.*

I will extol You, O Lord, for You have lifted me up from the pits of despair. You have broken the shackles of self-pity and given me victory through the battle.

> *The Lord thy God in the midst of thee is mighty;*
> *he will save,*
> *he will rejoice over thee with joy;*
> *he will rest in his love,*
> *he will joy over thee with singing.*

Wow! That is so hard to believe–that You could ever rejoice or sing over me! Your mercy is so amazing! I love you, Lord.

Zechariah 2:10   Isaiah 65:14   Zephaniah 3:17

UNCERTAIN REMISSION

Psalm 119:95 The wicked have waited for me to destroy me: but I will consider thy testimonies.

Remission. Sometimes the word sounds like music to my ears. But today it's not so comforting. Today I wonder if there are microscopic enemies–wicked cancer cells– lurking in my body, silently recruiting more mutinous cells before they attack my body again. With a vengeance.

If only I knew for sure. But these thoughts do me no good. They don't help me love You more, Lord. And they don't help me love others more. They don't give me joy. They nag at me, and they drag me down. Thinking like that is like going through life with the brakes on.

For thus saith the Lord God,
the Holy One of Israel;
In returning and rest shall ye be saved;
in quietness and in confidence
shall be your strength.

As an act of my will, and by Your grace, I will change my thought process. Instead of considering what might be going on in my body, I will consider Your testimonies. I will choose to believe and trust that, regardless of what happens, You know best.

I will consider all the promises You have communicated to me in the past. I will consider the countless answered prayers. I will consider the peace and hope that You have given me.

When the wicked lie in wait to ambush my thoughts, I will not be caught. I will think about You instead.

Isaiah 30:15

GIVE UP ON GOD

Psalm 119:115 Depart from me, ye evildoers: for I will keep the commandments of my God.

I have enough trouble with the taunts of the enemy within; why do people feel they have to bother me as well?

"Why do you still believe in God? Look what He's done to you," they say.

I feel like people are mocking You, Lord. I had such expectations that You'd just take this cancer away. But You didn't. Help me know how to respond. Help me to show love to people who try to tear my tattered faith to shreds.

Help me not to give in to the temptation to believe them. By Your grace alone I can be faithful to Your Word. But You've got to do Your part to help me keep on believing You, because I'm losing strength.

Blessed is the man that trusteth in the Lord,
and whose hope the Lord is.

Knowing that of the Lord
ye shall receive the reward of the inheritance:
for ye serve the Lord Christ.

And, behold, I come quickly;
and my reward is with me,
to give every man according as his work shall be.

Jeremiah 17:7   Colossians 3:24   Revelation 22:12

FACING ETERNITY

Psalm 63:4 Thus will I bless thee while I live: I will lift up my hands in thy name.

They say there's not much time left, Lord. But You already know that. Before I was even born, You knew that this day would come.

Yet I believe what Psalm 118:17 says: *"I shall not die, but live, and declare the works of the Lord."* This ol' body may die, but not me. I am going to live on through all eternity. And I'll have a glorified body, too, and disease will never be able to touch that body or work its wretched torture upon it.

For all eternity, I'll praise Your name. But right now, I'm a little frightened. What will happen to my family? How can I leave them? Who will . . . when I'm gone?

Know therefore that the Lord thy God,
he is God, the faithful God,
which keepeth covenant and mercy
with them that love him and keep his
commandments
to a thousand generations.

Oh, God, I need You! My family needs You!

The eternal God is thy refuge,
and underneath are the everlasting arms.

Precious in the sight of the Lord is the death
of his saints.

Deuteronomy 7:9   Deuteronomy 33:27   Psalm 116:15

HOLD ME UP

Psalm 119:117 Hold thou me up, and I shall be safe:
and I will have respect unto thy statutes continually.

Hold me up, Lord. I am so weak in so many ways.
Hold me up and let me live.

> *And call upon me in the day of trouble:*
> *I will deliver thee,*
> *and thou shalt glorify me.*

Don't let my footsteps slip, Lord.
Hold me up, and I know I will be safe.

> *The steps of a good man are ordered by the Lord:*
> *and he delighteth in his way.*
> *Though he fall,*
> *he shall not be utterly cast down:*
> *for the Lord upholdeth him with his hand.*

Psalm 50:15   Psalm 37:23-24

HELP FROM GOD'S WORD

Psalm 138:1-2 I will praise thee with my whole heart... I will worship toward thy holy temple, and praise thy name for thy lovingkindness and for thy truth: for thou hast magnified thy word above all thy name.

Ah, Lord, what would I do without the Bible? To me, my Bible is a treasure chest filled with immeasurable riches. It is a medicine cabinet filled with always-effective medications. It is a manual that tells me how to be forgiven and become a child of God. It is a wise counselor to give me answers and guidance. It is a source of sunlight to guide my path and brighten my day. It is a book of promises reserved for me.

The law of the Lord is perfect,
converting the soul:
the testimony of the Lord is sure,
making wise the simple.
The statutes of the Lord are right,
rejoicing the heart:
the commandment of the Lord is pure,
enlightening the eyes.
The fear of the Lord is clean,
enduring for ever:
the judgments of the Lord are true
and righteous altogether.
More to be desired are they than gold,
yea, than much fine gold:
sweeter also than honey and the honeycomb...
and in keeping of them
there is great reward.

Thank You for the ways we communicate through the written Word of God. Thank You for the love messages I get from You through Your word.

Thank You, my Friend, thank You. With my whole heart I thank You.

Psalm 19:7-11

WHILE I LIVE

Psalm 146:2 While I live will I praise the Lord: I will sing praises unto my God while I have any being.

Lord, I do not know what the future holds.
Only You know the time when You will call each of us to come to You.
Give me the grace I need to choose to praise You in the midst of the uncertainty.
While I have the ability to think and while I have breath, grant that I may always, only, choose to praise You.

Behold,

the eye of the Lord

is upon them that fear him,

upon them that hope in his mercy;

To deliver their soul

from death.

Psalm 33:18-19

YOU DID IT, LORD!

Psalm 52:9 I will praise thee for ever, because thou hast done it: and I will wait on thy name; for it is good before thy saints.

Hallelujah! You've done it, Lord! I thought this day would never come, but it is here. I am free!

I will praise You, because You are the one who has done it. I could never have gone through this without You.

Thank You, Lord. Thank You.

Behold,
I have refined thee,
but not with silver;
I have chosen thee in the furnace of affliction.
For mine own sake,
even for mine own sake...

For I know the thoughts that I think toward you,
saith the Lord,
thoughts of peace, and not of evil,
to give you an expected end.

Isaiah 48:10-11   Jeremiah 29:11

CHANGED AND AVAILABLE

Psalm 144:9 I will sing a new song unto thee, O God: upon a psaltery and an instrument of ten strings will I sing praises unto thee.

I'm a changed person, Lord. I'm not the same person I was when I first heard the diagnosis of cancer. There are so many ways in which I have changed, matured, grown wiser.

Life doesn't look the same as it did before. Even my relationships are changed. I need a renewed vision for what You have in mind for my future. I need You to give me a new song of my life to sing for Your glory.

Right now I can't imagine all that You have in mind, what doors You will open, what opportunities You will give me to be an encouragement to others who are going through this journey. But I don't need to know that now; all I need is the assurance that You will give me that new song to sing for You.

Therefore with joy
shall ye draw water out of the wells of salvation.
And in that day shall ye say,
Praise the Lord,
call upon his name,
declare his doings among the people,
make mention that his name is exalted.

I yield myself to You, fully and completely, to be who You want me to be, to do what You want me to do. Put a new song in my heart that I might sing praises to You and praise You with my life.

Isaiah 12:3-4

The Lord says,

"Because he hath set his love upon me,
therefore will I deliver him:
I will set him on high,
because he hath known my name.
He shall call upon me, and I will answer him:
I will be with him in trouble;
I will deliver him,
and honour him."

Psalm 91:14-15

Our Journey
through Cancer Land

Our Journey through Cancer Land

In the year of our Lord 2007, God allowed us to take part in one of His miracles. God chose to heal our thirteen-year-old daughter of a very aggressive form of non-Hodgkin lymphoma, Burkitt's type. In the process, we experienced a journey full of ups and downs; prayers and answers to prayers; pain, suffering, and joy. But most of all, we experienced God's presence and His blessings.

I suppose the story begins with the stray cat Sassy.

Jane had wanted a cat that would be a loyal, doting pet. She couldn't have a dog, so why not ask for a doglike cat, right? In the middle of July, a friend offered Jane a bedraggled, severely matted, on-death's-doorstep Siamese cat that a dog had found abandoned in the woods. Accepting our advice that a cat would be more likely to be attached to her if she nursed it back to health, Jane chose to adopt the dying cat. After a lot of Jane's tender loving care and several visits to the vet, the cat slowly regained its health.

A few weeks later, Jane had us feel the small almond-sized lump she'd found on the side of her neck. We made an appointment for her to see our primary care physician.

In early September, the doctor told us it was probably a swollen lymph node and discussed possible causes, including cat scratch disease because Sassy had recently joined our family. The doctor measured the lump carefully and scheduled a visit to recheck it if it didn't decrease in size in a month. Jane had no other symptoms, and her blood work came back normal. The doctor did mention the possibility of cancer, but, of course, we dismissed that.

The lump continued to increase in size so that by the time Jane returned to the doctor, the lump protruded visibly on her neck. Not only had the lump enlarged, it had also changed shape, spreading wider at the top. In retrospect, that probably indicated further lymph node involvement in the cancer.

In early October, the doctor measured the lump and immediately made an appointment with a surgeon for a biopsy. The doctor once again mentioned the possibility of lymphoma. Jane still had no other symptoms, but she cried quietly at the thought of losing her hair.

The next day Jane and I visited with the surgeon who performed an ultrasound and a biopsy (fine needle aspiration) in his office.

At that point we weren't too concerned. After all, statistics were in our favor–cancer in children is very rare. Even so, we began asking a few people to pray about the situation. In particular, we asked members of our church, Benton Bible Chapel, to pray. Our married daughter, Charity, asked her church to pray. Our good friends John and Shirley Donovan asked for prayer from their church family as well. Several people from their church knew Jane because she had recently joined its One Voice Choir.

About a week later we received a phone call with the pathology report, saying that the lymph node "appears benign," but "close clinical supervision is advised." At that point, the lump appeared to be getting smaller.

The next day the surgeon called to say he had decided to try a course of antibiotics, based on advice from other doctors. The consensus was that it was probably cat scratch fever even though there were no other symptoms. Jane began taking the antibiotics.

Later in the month Jane and I met with the surgeon again. The lump was smaller, but it was still there. The doctor still thought that it was probably a "reactive lymph node." However, he felt the right thing to do was to schedule a biopsy in the hospital. We still were not worried. After all, cancer doesn't just shrink on its own, right?

As the date approached for the biopsy, the lump continued to get smaller. I even wondered if when Jane went in for the biopsy, they might decide it was no longer necessary.

In the beginning of November, Jane had the biopsy at our local hospital. My husband, Jane, and I were all in good spirits that day, not too concerned about the outcome, fully expecting this procedure to be a mere formality.

The surgeon removed much of the lymph node, but he told us after the biopsy that the rest of the node was in too deep to reach with the small incision he had made. We understood why he didn't want to make a larger incision on a teenage girl's neck. He assured us that even if it were cancer, which he doubted, the treatment for that type of cancer does not involve surgery. Twice that day he told us that he removed only part of the node.

I asked him if I could see the lymph node that he had removed. I was just curious to see this thing. While Wayne was with Jane as she came out of the anesthesia, the doctor passed a small jar to me. It contained a dozen or so small, oddly cut up pieces of tissue in a clear fluid. He explained that he had had to take it out in pieces.

Jane bounced back fine, and a week later we received the results of the biopsy. Our primary care physician walked into the examining room where Jane and I were waiting and told the two of us that the pathology report indicated non-Hodgkin lymphoma, Burkitt's type. We were surprised. Jane cried quietly while I hugged her. Her greatest concern was that she didn't want to lose her hair. I was somewhat numb because I really wasn't expecting this news.

Although some might question the way the doctor broke the news, I wouldn't have had her do it any other way.

After telling Wayne the news and receiving his support, Jane and I went to her sister Charity's house. There, Jane had a fun diversion from the diagnosis, and I had the opportunity to use her faster Internet connection to send an e-mail to people, asking them to pray.

That evening a doctor at Dartmouth-Hitchcock Medical Center (DHMC) called and talked with me for 45 minutes. She scheduled a battery of tests for two days later. It was sobering to hear her describe the anticipated course of treatment.

Burkitt's is an aggressive, fast-growing cancer. One of Jane's hematologist oncologists said she had seen a tumor double in size in forty-eight hours. I think I saw the fast-growing side of Burkitt's in September before anyone was asked to pray about it. The lump had gotten much bigger by the time we went for the follow-up visit a month later. However, the lump did not continue to grow. After the possibility of NHL was mentioned and several churches began to pray for healing, the lump definitely began to shrink.

In mid-November intense testing began. Jane had blood drawn, a spinal tap, a bone aspiration, a bone marrow test, and a CT scan. These procedures were a harrowing experience, but the staff at DHMC helped to make it more bearable for Jane.

Preliminary results from the tests were inconclusive: either Stage I or Stage III. The doctors found no evidence of cancer, even in her neck where part of the lymph node/tumor had been left behind. There was only one questionable area in her chest cavity that could have been her thymus gland or a tumor. Jane was scheduled for a PET scan the following Tuesday.

Because of the unusual findings, the hospital sent for the tissue sample from the biopsy in order to retest it. DHMC confirmed the original diagnosis of non-Hodgkin lymphoma, Burkitt's type.

The following week, the PET scan confirmed the diagnosis: Stage I cancer. Yet to the doctors' amazement, there was no visible cancer anywhere in her body—even in her neck! That is an awesome tribute to God at work.

The doctors said that the surgeon must have done a great job removing all of the tumor during the biopsy, but the surgeon specifically told us that he had not removed the entire node.

Praise God for His divine intervention!

We praised God for healing Jane, but we found ourselves in an unusual position. It appeared that God had healed Jane of cancer, but the doctors still wanted her to undergo chemotherapy, including spinal chemotherapy.

We said no thanks, because God has healed her. But the doctors felt compelled to refer us to an Ethics Committee to determine whether we were competent to make that decision or whether we were acting in the best interests of our child.

We decided to form our own "ethics committee" of sorts. We contacted many different believers who had had various involvements with cancer and asked their opinion. The general consensus of that group was that we should go through with chemo, especially because at Stage I the treatment would last only about 10 weeks.

It was an agonizing decision, but in the end we decided to follow the doctors' advice and allow Jane to go through chemo.

After much prayer and searching for God's wisdom and leading, we based our decision upon this question: "What if we are wrong?"

If we were to choose not to have her go through chemo, and we were wrong because there were still microscopic cancer cells in her body, then the end result would be major chemotherapy and possibly more drastic treatments due to the fast-growing nature of Burkitt's.

If we chose to have her go through chemo and this was the wrong decision because God had already healed her, the end result would be that she underwent the agony of chemo for less than three months and gained valuable experiences for empathizing with others. We did consider the possibility of long-term side effects, but because of the low dosage of the chemo and the short duration of the treatment, we decided we could accept that risk.

Jane's brother and sister-in-law were helpful in encouraging us at this stage. "If God was able to protect her through cancer," Tim and Codie pointed out, "then God is able to protect her through chemo." And that is just what He did.

Jane began her first chemo treatment at the end of November, and her last treatment was in early February of 2008. She suffered with the typical side effects of nausea, vomiting, horrible headaches, weird tastes in her mouth, dry mouth, insomnia, and other assorted unpleasantries. Despite this, she maintained a surprisingly peaceful and cooperative attitude most of the time. (Admittedly, she didn't do so well with the doctors–she saw them as the "enemy." But she loved all of the other staff members at DHMC.) In general, we were awed by her graceful acceptance of the situation.

Despite having to deal with these physical problems, Jane escaped other major side effects. Throughout the course of chemo, her blood counts were high. The technician once described the blood counts as "fantastic." Her doctors described them as "spectacular" and "continue to be spectacular."

Jane never had any of the expected setbacks from chemo. We were able to stay on the original schedule. In fact, at Christmas time when the rest of the family was sick with a wretched, long-lasting virus, Jane appeared to be the healthiest one of all!

On top of that, God also protected Jane's hair. One doctor said that everyone lost all of their hair with this particular type of chemo. Before treatment began, Jane got a haircut and donated her long, thick brown hair to Locks of Love. She originally intended to cut the rest off when it started to fall out, but she chose not to do that. She said so many people told her that they were praying for her not to lose all of her hair, that she kept it for them. Throughout the treatments, Jane's hair thinned out considerably, but she still retained more than enough so that when she wore her winter hat, her hair looked "normal." When she completed chemo, we cut off her remaining hair to allow the new hair to grow evenly. Interestingly, her hair began to grow back as a lovely ash blond.

When I asked one of her doctors about Jane's unusual progress, the doctor said, "I believe in miracles!"

We were surprised to hear her describe Jane's progress as a miracle because we had watched Jane suffer in so many ways. But to a doctor who deals with treatments for life-threatening diseases every day, Jane's situation was undoubtedly a miracle.

Truly, God protected her during her chemo treatments.

In early February Jane went for her last treatment. There was no need to do any testing to see if the cancer was gone, because, as the doctor said, there was no visible cancer when they began treatment.

After the completion of the treatments, our church, Benton Bible Chapel, put on a victory celebration for Jane using butterflies and bubbles as their theme. Bubbles remind us of the joys and yet the fleeting nature of our life here on earth. And, of course, the butterflies symbolized the new life Jane was granted here on earth. In heaven, we'll see the real fulfillment of the transformation the butterfly represents.

Our Journey through Cancer Land was brief compared to most other people's experiences with cancer, but it was a life-changing experience nonetheless. The girl who lives in our home with us now is not the same girl we started with. Those few months have refined and matured her. Her father and I are not the same either. The experience has opened our eyes to a whole new way of viewing things.

And one more thing: Remember that stray cat that Jane wanted to be like a dog? The cat who had recently gone through its own health struggles returned Jane's tender-loving care. Sassy stayed by Jane's side throughout the ordeal. Whether lying quietly beside her on the recliner sofa, or following her and waiting outside the bathroom door or being her faithful companion at her bedside, Sassy was always there for her. And nearly every time Jane returned home after being away, the cat greeted her at the door.

Months later we learned another aspect of God's handiwork in this situation. We were looking up information about Siamese cats on the Internet, and we were surprised to find a description that matched not just our cat's looks, but matched its personality perfectly. Sassy is apparently a California Ragdoll–a cat that is sometimes described as a "puppy-cat" because of its doglike qualities. Isn't God amazing? God really did provide a cat that would be like a dog for Jane!

Our loving God used the prayers of many brothers and sisters in Christ to help bring about unforgettable miracles in our lives. We will be eternally grateful for those prayers.

We are grateful for the many people who have prayed for Jane, and some who continue to pray for her. We are grateful for the many people who have prayed for us, as well. We feel blessed– extremely blessed– and we are thankful.

We do not understand why God chose to heal Jane while others are not healed of cancer. Our hearts go out to people whose Journey through Cancer Land is infinitely longer and more challenging than our journey. And we pray that this book will be a source of comfort and strength to those in the Journey and to those who walk along beside them.

Am I a Child of God?
How Can I Know for Sure I Will
Go to Heaven?

Am I a Child of God?

How do I become a child of God? How can I know for sure that when I leave this earth that I will go to heaven to live with Jesus?

To become a child of God and to live a life that is pleasing to God, earnestly, prayerfully apply the following guidelines from the Word of God:

Come to the point of realizing and accepting that there is no way any of us will ever be good enough to earn our way to heaven.

Have a desire to yield your life to God.

Indicate to the Lord that you understand that you have sinned.

Look to Jesus and the sacrifice He made by dying on the cross for you, and believe He paid the penalty for your sins.

Decide to ask Him to forgive you for all of your sins, and ask Him to be your Savior.

Offer your life to God.

Find someone you can tell about your decision.

Grab onto God's promises that when you yield your life to Him, acknowledge that Jesus is God, and ask for His forgiveness, you become a child of God.

Openly accept and believe that when you asked Him to be your Savior, He said, "YES!" and you were born again into the family of God.

Determine to study your Bible and learn all you can so you can grow and mature as a Believer, and so you can be able to enjoy all the benefits of your life as a child of God here on earth.

Let's look at each of those points more closely with the help of the Bible.

Come to the point of realizing and accepting that there is no way any of us will ever be good enough to earn our way to heaven.

Ephesians 2:8-9 For by grace are ye saved through faith; and that not of yourselves: it is the gift of God: Not of works, lest any man should boast.

Romans 3:24 Being justified freely by his [God's] grace through the redemption that is in Christ Jesus.

Ephesians 1:6-7 To the praise of the glory of his [God's] grace, wherein he hath made us accepted in the beloved. In whom we have redemption through his blood, the forgiveness of sins, according to the riches of his grace.

Have a desire to yield your life to God.

Revelation 3:20 [Jesus says,] Behold, I stand at the door, and knock: if any man hear my voice, and open the door, I will come in to him, and will sup with him, and he with me.

2 Corinthians 6:2 For he [God] saith, I have heard thee in a time accepted, and in the day of salvation have I [helped] thee: behold, now is the accepted time; behold, now is the day of salvation.

Indicate to the Lord that you understand that you have sinned.

Romans 3:10 As it is written, There is none righteous, no, not one.

Romans 3:23 For all have sinned, and come short of the glory of God.

Look to Jesus and the sacrifice He made by dying on the cross, and believe He paid the penalty for your sins.

Romans 6:23 For the wages of sin is death; but the gift of God is eternal life through Jesus Christ our Lord.

Romans 5:8 But God commendeth his love toward us, in that, while we were yet sinners, Christ died for us.

Titus 3:5-7 Not by works of righteousness which we have done, but according to his mercy he saved us, by the washing of regeneration, and renewing of the Holy Ghost; Which he shed on us abundantly through Jesus Christ our Saviour; That being justified by his [God's] grace, we should be made heirs according to the hope of eternal life.

Decide to ask Him to forgive you for all of your sins and ask Him to be your Savior.

Hosea 14:2 Take with you words, and turn to the Lord: say unto him, Take away all iniquity, and receive us graciously.

Romans 10:13 For whosoever shall call upon the name of the Lord shall be saved.

Ephesians 1:5-7 Having predestinated us unto the adoption of children by Jesus Christ to himself, according to the good pleasure of his will, To the praise of the glory of his grace, wherein he hath made us accepted in the beloved. In whom we have redemption through his blood, the forgiveness of sins, according to the riches of his grace.

Acts 3:19 Repent ye therefore, and be converted, that your sins may be blotted out, when the times of refreshing shall come from the presence of the Lord.

Acts 10:43 To him [Jesus] give all the prophets witness, that through his name whosoever believeth in him shall receive remission of sins.

Offer your life to God.

2 Corinthians 5:14-15 For the love of Christ constraineth us; because we thus judge, that if one died for all, then were all dead: And that he died for all, that they which live should not henceforth live unto themselves, but unto him which died for them, and rose again.

Romans 12:1-2 I beseech you therefore, brethren, by the mercies of God, that ye present your bodies a living sacrifice, holy, acceptable unto God, which is your reasonable service. And be not conformed to this world: but be ye transformed by the renewing of your mind, that ye may prove what is that good, and acceptable, and perfect, will of God.

Find someone you can tell about your decision.

Romans 10:9-10 That if thou shalt confess with thy mouth the Lord Jesus, and shalt believe in thine heart that God hath raised him from the dead, thou shalt be saved. For with the heart man believeth unto righteousness; and with the mouth confession is made unto salvation.

Luke 12:8 [Jesus says,] Also I say unto you, Whosoever shall confess me before men, him shall the Son of man also confess before the angels of God.

Grab onto God's promises that when you yield your life to Him, acknowledge that Jesus is God, and ask for His forgiveness, you become a child of God.

John 1:12-13 But as many as received him [Jesus], to them gave he power to become the sons of God, even to them that believe on his name: Which were born, not of blood, nor of the will of the flesh, nor of the will of man, but of God.

1 Timothy 2:3-6 For this is good and acceptable in the sight of God our Saviour; Who will have all men to be saved, and to come unto the knowledge of the truth. For there is one God, and one mediator between God and men, the man Christ Jesus; Who gave himself a ransom for all...

1 John 3:1-2 Behold, what manner of love the Father hath bestowed upon us, that we should be called the sons of God: therefore the world knoweth us not, because it knew him not. Beloved, now are we the sons of God, and it doth not yet appear what we shall be: but we know that, when he shall appear, we shall be like him; for we shall see him as he is.

Openly accept and believe that when you asked Him to be your Savior, He said, "YES!" and you were born again into the family of God.

1 John 1:9 If we confess our sins, he [Jesus] is faithful and just to forgive us our sins, and to cleanse us from all unrighteousness.

Ephesians 2:4-5 But God, who is rich in mercy, for his great love wherewith he loved us, Even when we were dead in sins, hath quickened us together with Christ, (by grace ye are saved).

Colossians 2:13 And you, being dead in your sins and the uncircumcision of your flesh, hath he [Jesus] quickened together with him, having forgiven you all trespasses.

1 John 2:12 I write unto you, little children, because your sins are forgiven you for his name's sake.

1 John 5:11-13 And this is the record, that God hath given to us eternal life, and this life is in his Son. He that hath the Son hath life; and he that hath not the Son of God hath not life. These things have I written unto you that believe on the name of the Son of God; that ye may know that ye have eternal life, and that ye may believe on the name of the Son of God.

Determine to study your Bible and learn all you can so you can grow and mature as a Believer, and so you can be able to enjoy all the benefits of your life as a child of God here on earth.

2 Timothy 2:15 Study to shew thyself approved unto God, a workman that needeth not to be ashamed, rightly dividing the word of truth.

1 Peter 2:2-3 As newborn babes, desire the sincere milk of the word [the Bible], that ye may grow thereby: If so be ye have tasted that the Lord is gracious.

Psalm 19:7-10 The law of the Lord is perfect, converting the soul: the testimony of the Lord is sure, making wise the simple. The statutes of the Lord are right, rejoicing the heart: the commandment of the Lord is pure, enlightening the eyes. The fear of the Lord is clean, enduring for ever: the judgments of the Lord are true and righteous altogether. More to be desired are they than gold, yea, than much fine gold: sweeter also than honey and the honeycomb.

2 Corinthians 5:17 Therefore if any man be in Christ, he is a new creature: old things are passed away; behold, all things are become new.

Romans 8:11 But if the Spirit of him that raised up Jesus from the dead dwell in you, he that raised up Christ from the dead shall also quicken your mortal bodies by his Spirit that dwelleth in you.

Psalm 16:11 Thou [the Lord] wilt shew me the path of life: in thy [God's] presence is fulness of joy; at thy right hand there are pleasures for evermore.

~ ~ ~ ~ ~ ~ ~

Here is a sample of the type of prayer that you can pray. Remember, it is not the specific words that you say that will make you a child of God. As you pray, it is the belief in your heart and your sincere desire to give your life to Jesus, asking Him to be your Savior that enables you to be born again into the family of God.

Dear Heavenly Father,

I know I have sinned and that I am not worthy to come into Your presence on my own. I know I have sinned, and Your Word says that the wages or penalty of sin is death–eternal separation from You. But I believe that Jesus, the Son of God, died in my place to pay the penalty for my sins. I ask You to forgive me for all my sins. I ask You, Jesus, to be my Savior and take me to heaven with you when I die. I give my life to you.

Thank you for dying for my sins, Jesus. Thank you for accepting me into Your family as a Child of God. Thank you for cleansing me from all sins. Thank you for giving me a fresh new start. Amen.

Who Is This God That I Love?

Who Is This God That I Love?

Who is this God that I love? He is who He says He is. He is the

God of Heaven and the Whole Earth.

He is the One in supreme command over all angelic forces. He is the

God of Hosts.

He is sovereign over fallen angels and their leader, the god of this world, for He is the

God of gods.

Yet He is not only supreme over the spiritual realm; He is sovereign over the physical world, because He is the

God of All Flesh.

Unlike our enemy who comes to steal and kill and destroy, our God has sent His Son that we might have eternal life for He is the

God of the Living.

Yes, He is the God of heaven and earth, the God of hosts, the God of gods, and the God of all flesh. He is all-powerful, all-knowing, and always present. But don't let His omnipotence, omniscience, and omnipresence lead you to think He is a distant, impersonal God. No, He is the

God of Love.

And because He is the God of Love, He is a personal God. He is the

God of My Life
God of My Mercy and the
God of My Strength.

Through all the trials and struggles of life, He is the

God of My Rock.

The God of My Rock is a source of shade from the sweltering sun; He's my shelter and security from my enemies. To some a rock is hard, unyielding; it is true that God is the

God of Judgment.

And in God's time He will bring judgment upon those who reject Him. But that is only one facet of who He is.

So why does this Rock not crush me? Because He is the

God of Truth and Knowledge.

He knows me exactly as I am. He knows that on my own I could never, ever merit His approval or blessings. That is why this God of Love, the

God of Our Lord Jesus Christ,

sent His only begotten Son into the world to become the

God of My Salvation.

He is the God of my salvation, and the salvation of all who will humble themselves to confess that Jesus is Lord, and to ask His forgiveness.

So who is this God that I love?

He is all I have said, and more. He is the

God of Peace

God of Hope

God of Patience

God of All Comfort

God of All Grace.

Praise be to His Name! Truly,

He is the God of Glory!

Breinigsville, PA USA
01 April 2010
235280BV00002B/2/P